SEEDLIP

THE COCKTAIL BOOK

SEEDLIP

THE COCKTAIL BOOK

100 DELICIOUS
NON-ALCOHOLIC RECIPES
FROM SEEDLIP &
THE WORLD'S BEST BARS

BANTAM PRESS

LONDON · NEW YORK · TORONTO · SYDNEY · AUCKLAND

TRANSWORLD PUBLISHERS
61–63 Uxbridge Road, London W5 5SA
www.penguin.co.uk

Transworld is part of the Penguin Random House group of companies
whose addresses can be found at global.penguinrandomhouse.com

First published in Great Britain in 2018 by Bantam Press
an imprint of Transworld Publishers

A CIP catalogue record for this book
is available from the British Library.

ISBN 9781787630109

Designed and typeset in Brown & Baskerville/11pt by Smith & Gilmour
Printed and bound in China by C&C Offset Printing Co., Ltd.

Penguin Random House is committed to a sustainable
future for our business, our readers and our planet. This book
is made from Forest Stewardship Council® certified paper.

1 3 5 7 9 10 8 6 4 2

CONTENTS

INTRODUCTION 6

—

SPICE 94 12
LONG & SHORT COCKTAILS 16
GUEST COCKTAILS 42

—

GARDEN 108 68
LONG & SHORT COCKTAILS 72
GUEST COCKTAILS 98

—

GROVE 42 124
LONG & SHORT COCKTAILS 128
GUEST COCKTAILS 156

—

SHRUBS & SYRUPS 170
GLOSSARY 184
INDEX 188

WHAT IS SEEDLIP?

Seedlip is a nature company on a mission to change the way the world drinks by solving the *what to drink when you're not drinking* dilemma with the world's first distilled non-alcoholic spirits.

Served in the best restaurants, bars & hotels in the world, Seedlip is inspired by Ben Branson's family's 300-year farming heritage & *The Art of Distillation*, a book written in 1651 detailing the distilled non-alcoholic herbal remedies produced by apothecaries.

The three Seedlip spirits – Spice 94, Garden 108 & Grove 42 – are blended & bottled in England. Seedlip has created a bespoke maceration, copper pot distillation & filtration process for each plant to capture & celebrate the true flavours of nature. All three Seedlip spirits are free from not only alcohol, but also sugar, sweeteners, calories & allergens, making them the ideal grown-up option if you're not drinking – whatever the reason.

WELCOME

Thank you for buying *The Seedlip Cocktail Book*.

We launched Seedlip back in November 2015. I'd been working on Seedlip for over two years, bringing together things I'm passionate about – nature, farming, design & ingredients – into a bottle. I knew that the *what to drink when you're not drinking* dilemma needed solving & hoped others would share my view that it was time for the world of non-alcoholic drinks to be taken seriously. Thankfully, I have since come across so many wonderful people who share that vision & who are helping us to change the way the world drinks.

This book is a celebration of nature through some of our favorite recipes & recipes from some of the world's best bartenders. It's not for your coffee table; it's for folded corners, scribbles, tatty pages & Post-its. There are simple recipes & simple techniques; really fiddly recipes & some really unusual gadgets[1]; everyday, ordinary ingredients & forgotten, rare ones, too.

Whether you're a professional bartender or an at-home experimenter, I hope these pages demonstrate that cocktails without alcohol, when taken seriously, can be both delicious & a lot of fun[2].

Peas & love

Ben

[1] Do refer to the glossary at the back when in doubt!
[2] The guest recipes are trickier. They highlight just how creative we've been getting with Seedlip & offer an opportunity for more experienced bartenders to experiment!

FIVE FACTS ABOUT SEEDLIP

1

A seedlip is a seed sower's basket. Seedlips were used
by Ben's family over 300 years ago to hand-sow seed.

2

Carolus Linnaeus – the 'godfather of botany' – gave 4,000
animals their Latin names, including the fox, the hare & the
squirrel that feature on the front of Seedlip's bottles.

3

Some of Ben's ancestors' initials are hidden in the fox
illustration on Spice 94.

4

Seedlip is the proud owner of a copy of *The Art of Distillation*
that dates back to 1664. The original copy can
be found in the British Library & used to belong
to King George III.

5

The first 1,000 bottles of Seedlip sold out in 3 weeks,
the second in 3 days & the third in just 30 minutes.

OUR APPROACH TO COCKTAILS

In bars, restaurants & hotels, the back-bars brim with alcoholic options. And there are hundreds of years of tried & tested recipes using these ingredients. So, with a wealth of books, websites & home barware to experiment with, it has never been easier to have a go at home.

However, proper non-alcoholic cocktails are new. There aren't lots of products, recipes & information. And this is what makes it so exciting. The limitations – creativity's greatest ally – are actually very liberating. There are no established 'ways' to make non-alcoholic cocktails; there aren't any 'classics' yet; there have not been 100 years of 'this is how it must be made'. Instead, there is an opportunity to create the classic Seedlip cocktails of the future.

We like to approach each Seedlip cocktail as a chef approaches a plate of food, pairing great ingredients in interesting ways to produce fantastic flavours. The three distinct flavour profiles of Spice 94, Garden 108 & Grove 42 complement different plants & different combinations. Once we have a combination in mind (for example, Spice 94 with ginger & cashew, or Garden 108 with basil & strawberry), we can then explore the best techniques, the right quantities, the ideal glassware, what kind of ice, what garnish &, of course, what we're going to call it!

INGREDIENTS & PAIRINGS

Here are some examples of ingredients & food pairings that work particularly well with each of the three Seedlip flavours.

SPICE 94

Complementary Ingredients: Grapefruit, Pineapple, Vanilla, Maple, Cinnamon, Coffee
Can be paired with: Red Meat, Root Veg, Curries, Desserts, Petits Fours

GARDEN 108

Complementary Ingredients: Apple, Rhubarb, Basil, Cucumber, Elderflower, Lime
Can be paired with: Starters, White Fish, Salads, Palate Cleansers, Sorbets

GROVE 42

Complementary Ingredients: Peanut, Carrot, Barley, Ginger, Honey, Apricot
Can be paired with: Paté, Spicy Dishes, Shellfish, Game, Chocolate-based Desserts

THE EIGHT TENETS FOR NON-ALCOHOLIC COCKTAILS

Here are some principles we abide by when creating drinks.

1
G.I.G. [GLASS. ICE. GARNISH.]
Smart glass, lots of ice
& don't forget the garnish.

2
THINK LIKE A CHEF
Think flavour & ingredients first,
then the delivery.

3
REUSE, REDUCE, RECYCLE
Syrups, shrubs, ferments, jams
& salts are all handy ways to reduce
your waste & add a real depth of
flavour to non-alcoholic cocktails.
Make sure to reuse produce or
recycle ingredients.

4
STAY SEASONAL (WHERE POSSIBLE)
Being in tune with the rhythm
of the seasons & your climate feels
better, tastes better & is better
for the environment.

5
STAY LOCAL (WHERE POSSIBLE)
Find your local farm shop or
'pick-your-own' farm, grow your own
or check out some of the amazing fruit
& veg box services available.

6
'ROOT TO SHOOT'
We're all familiar with nose to tail
or farm to table, 'root to shoot' is our
Seedlip equivalent. The stone, the peel,
the leaves, the flowers – all are tasty
in their own right.

7
HOST WITH THE MOST
One of the most powerful ways to
delight guests & truly be the perfect host
is to prioritize your guests' experience &
consider their individual requirements.
Whether that means taking into
account someone's allergy or that
someone is driving or vegetarian –
leave no one out.

8
NO MOCKING
The word *mocktails* is an insult! Let's talk about *Seedlip
cocktails* or *non-alcoholic cocktails* instead. Please.

PROFILE

Aromatic & Complex

PLANTS

Allspice Berries
Green Cardamom
Oak
Cascarilla Bark
Grapefruit Peel
Lemon Peel

FREE FROM

No Sugar
No Sweetener
No Allergens

SEEDLIP

—

SPICE 94

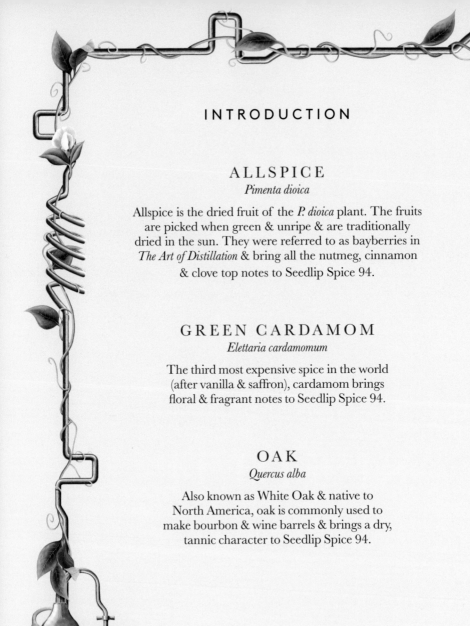

INTRODUCTION

ALLSPICE
Pimenta dioica

Allspice is the dried fruit of the *P. dioica* plant. The fruits
are picked when green & unripe & are traditionally
dried in the sun. They were referred to as bayberries in
The Art of Distillation & bring all the nutmeg, cinnamon
& clove top notes to Seedlip Spice 94.

GREEN CARDAMOM
Elettaria cardamomum

The third most expensive spice in the world
(after vanilla & saffron), cardamom brings
floral & fragrant notes to Seedlip Spice 94.

OAK
Quercus alba

Also known as White Oak & native to
North America, oak is commonly used to
make bourbon & wine barrels & brings a dry,
tannic character to Seedlip Spice 94.

CASCARILLA
Croton eluteria

Native to the Caribbean, the bark from cascarilla is highly aromatic with sweet, nutty notes on the palate. It has historically been used in vermouth & *amaro*.

GRAPEFRUIT
Citrus × paradisi

Originating in Barbados from an accidental cross between a sweet orange & a pomelo, grapefruits were introduced to Europe in the 17th century. The oils in the peel bring a fantastic bitterness & an adult tart character to Seedlip Spice 94.

LEMON
Citrus × limon

Lemon entered Europe via Italy no later than the 2nd century during the time of Ancient Rome. Wonderfully fragrant, rich in terpenes & tannins, the peel has a sour acidity & delivers that fresh zesty character.

MENU

LONG COCKTAILS
—
ALL THE SPICE
GINGER
ELIZA
SPICE BOOCH
VANILLA
PUMPKIN
PINEAPPLE

SHORT COCKTAILS
—
NODDY
ESPRESSO MARTI**NO**
SPICE MARTI**NO**
MR HOWARD
NOGRONI

SPICE 94
LONG COCKTAILS · SHORT COCKTAILS

CHAPTER
1

ALL THE SPICE

SPICE 94 · TONIC/SODA · GRAPEFRUIT

—

Christopher Columbus discovered allspice berries in Jamaica in 1494.

INGREDIENTS
—

Spice 94: 50ml
Tonic/Soda: Top
Ice: Cubed
Garnish: Grapefruit Twist
Glass: Tall

METHOD
—

Fill a tall glass with ice

Add Spice 94

Top with tonic or soda

Garnish with a grapefruit twist

GINGER

—

The ancient Greeks ate ginger wrapped in bread. They eventually decided to add ginger to the bread & gingerbread was born.

INGREDIENTS

—

Spice 94: 50ml
Ginger Ale: Top
Ice: Cubed
Garnish: Orange Disc
Glass: Tumbler

METHOD

—

Fill a tumbler with ice

Add Spice 94

Top with ginger ale

Garnish with an orange disc

ELIZA

SPICE 94 · MARMALADE · CASSIA

—

*This recipe is a tribute to Madam Eliza Cholmondeley whose
1677 recipe book featured one of the earliest marmalade recipes.*

INGREDIENTS

—

Spice 94: 50ml
Marmalade: 1 tsp
Soda: Top
Ice: Cubed
Garnish: Charred Cassia Bark
Glass: Jam Jar

METHOD

—

Add Spice 94 & marmalade to a shaker with ice

Shake for 30 seconds

Strain into a jam jar

To char the cassia bark, light the end until it begins to smoke

Garnish with charred cassia bark

SPICE BOOCH

SPICE 94 · KOMBUCHA · LEMON

—

Kombucha has 80 other names worldwide, including Zaubertrank, which is German for 'magic potion'.

INGREDIENTS

—

Spice 94: 50ml
Royal Flush Real Kombucha (*see page 186*): Top
Ice: Cubed
Garnish: Lemon Twist
Glass: Tumbler

METHOD

—

Fill a tumbler with ice

Add Spice 94

Top with Kombucha

Garnish with a lemon twist

VANILLA

SPICE 94 · VANILLA · APPLE

—

*According to popular belief, the Totonac people from the
east coast of Mexico were the first to cultivate vanilla.*

INGREDIENTS

—

Spice 94: 50ml
Vanilla Extract: 1 tsp
Soda: Top
Ice: Cubed
Garnish: Green Apple Slice
Glass: Tumbler

METHOD

—

Fill a tumbler with ice

Add Spice 94 & vanilla extract

Top with soda

Garnish with a slice of green apple

PUMPKIN

—

Pumpkins are actually a fruit from the Cucurbitaceae family.
Other members include cucumbers & certain melons.

INGREDIENTS

—

Spice 94: 50ml
Ginger & Pumpkin Shrub (*see page 64*): 2 tbsp
Soda: Top
Ice: Cut Block
Garnish: Lemon Twist
Glass: Tall

METHOD

—

Fill a tall glass with ice

Add Spice 94 & Ginger & Pumpkin Shrub & stir

Top with soda

Garnish with a lemon twist

PINEAPPLE

SPICE 94 · LIME · PINEAPPLE · SAGE

It can take up to 3 years for a single pineapple to mature &, once harvested, it stops ripening.

INGREDIENTS

Spice 94: 50ml
Fresh Lime Juice: 1 tsp
Pineapple Tepache (*see page 67*): 80ml
Ice: Cubed
Garnish: Sage Leaf
Glass: Tumbler

METHOD

Fill a tumbler with ice

Add Spice 94 & lime juice

Top with Pineapple Tepache

Garnish with a sage leaf

NODDY

—

January 11th is National Hot Toddy Day &
June 21st is International Gnome Day.

INGREDIENTS

—

Spice 94: 50ml
Fresh Lemon Juice: 1 tbsp
Manuka Honey: 1 tbsp
Boiling Water: Top
Garnish: Lemon Wheel
Glass: Mug

METHOD

—

Add Spice 94, lemon juice & honey to a mug

Top with boiling water & stir

Garnish with a lemon wheel

ESPRESSO MARTI**NO**

SPICE 94 · COFFEE

—

A young goat herder first discovered coffee in Ethiopia circa AD*800.*

INGREDIENTS
—

Spice 94: 50ml
Sandows Cold Brew Concentrate (*see page 186*): 50ml
Sugar Syrup (*see page 186*): 1 tbsp
Ice: Cubed
Garnish: 3 Coffee Beans
Glass: Coupe

METHOD
—

Add Spice 94, Sandows Cold Brew Concentrate
& Sugar Syrup to a shaker

Add ice & shake

Double strain into a coupe glass

Garnish with 3 coffee beans

SPICE MARTI**NO**

SPICE 94 · VERJUS · OLIVE

—

Verjus is the juice of unripe white grapes. The word derives from the middle French vert jus, *meaning 'green juice'.*

INGREDIENTS
—

Spice 94: 60ml
Verjus (White Grape Juice): 2 tsp
Olive Brine: 1 tsp
Ice: Cubed
Garnish: Nocellara Olive
Glass: Coupe

METHOD
—

Add ice to a mixing glass with the Spice 94,
verjus & olive brine

Stir for 45 seconds

Strain into a coupe glass

Garnish with a Nocellara olive

MR HOWARD
SPICE 94 · GRAPEFRUIT · LEMON · STAR ANISE
—

This cocktail is named after Stewart Howard,
one of the first people in the world to serve Seedlip.

INGREDIENTS
—

Spice 94: 50ml
Fresh Pink Grapefruit Juice: 2 tbsp
Fresh Lemon Juice: 20ml
Sugar Syrup (*see page 186*): 1 tbsp
Ice: Cubed
Garnish: Star Anise
Glass: Coupe

METHOD
—

Add Spice 94, grapefruit juice, lemon juice
& sugar syrup to a shaker with ice

Shake for 30 seconds

Double strain into a coupe glass

Garnish with a star anise

NOGRONI®

—

*This drink was born in Ben Branson's garage & debuted
at The World's 50 Best Bar Awards in London in 2017.*

INGREDIENTS
—

Spice 94: 35ml
Non-alcoholic Bitter Aperitif (*see page 64*): 25ml
Non-alcoholic Sweet Vermouth (*see page 64*): 25ml
Ice: Block
Garnish: Orange Twist
Glass: Tumbler

METHOD
—

Add ice to a tumbler

Pour in the Spice 94, Bitter Aperitif & Sweet Vermouth

Stir for 20 seconds

Garnish with an orange twist

MENU
—
MELONDRAMATIC
COCANELA
SOMETHING IN THE WAY
SPICE & EVERYTHING NICE
PAIS DE LA CANELA
BREEZE FIELD
WINTER SHANDY
ROOT CELLAR
TALLSTRUNT
SOUVERIAN

SPICE 94

GUEST COCKTAILS

A selection of cocktails from some of the world's best bartenders

CHAPTER
2

MELONDRAMATIC

SPICE 94 · KOLA · WATERMELON · LEMON MYRTLE

—

MICHAEL CHIEM & THOR BERGQUIST– PS40, SYDNEY

Cocktail Bar of the Year 2018 – Time Out Australia

INGREDIENTS

—

Spice 94: 50ml
Kola Nut Tea (*see page 64*): 25ml
Rectified Watermelon Juice (*see page 65*): 25ml
PS Lemon Myrtle Soda (*see page 186*): 60ml
Ice: Cubed
Garnish: Watermelon Ball & Watermelon Rind Dust
Glass: Tumbler

METHOD

—

Add all the ingredients to a tumbler over ice

Garnish with a watermelon ball

Toast the skin of the watermelon with a blowtorch,
then grate the toasted part over the top

COCANELA

SPICE 94 · COCONUT · HONEY · LEMON · CINNAMON

—

DEV JOHNSON – EMPLOYEES ONLY, NEW YORK CITY
37th Best Bar in the World – World's 50 Best Bar Awards 2017

INGREDIENTS
—

Spice 94: 60ml
Coconut Milk: 2 tbsp
Honey Syrup (*see page 185*): 20ml
Fresh Lemon Juice: 1 tbsp
Sugar Syrup (*see page 186*): 1 tbsp
Ice: Crushed
Garnish: Grated Cinnamon
Glass: Tall

METHOD
—

Add all the ingredients to a tall glass & fill with crushed ice

Gently mix with a bar spoon

Grate cinnamon over the top to garnish

SOMETHING
IN THE WAY
SPICE 94 · FAUX VERMOUTH · MAPLE

—

ROBIN GOODFELLOW – PRETTY UGLY & BAR RAVAL, TORONTO
Both Bars were Top 10 Canada Cocktail Bars 2018 – Canada's 100 Best Bar & Restaurant Awards

INGREDIENTS
—

Spice 94: 45ml
Maple Faux Vermouth (*see page 65*): 45ml
Ice: Large Clear Block
Garnish: Maple Leaf
Glass: Tumbler

METHOD
—

Add all the ingredients to a tumbler

Garnish with a maple leaf

SPICE &
EVERYTHING NICE

SPICE 94 · CHAMOMILE · PINK PEPPERCORN · PEAR

—

NICOLAS TORRES – LAZY BEAR, SAN FRANCISCO

2 Michelin Stars – Michelin Guide 2017

INGREDIENTS

—

Spice 94: 45ml
Heavy-steeped Chamomile Tea: 2 tbsp
Pink Peppercorn Gum Syrup (*see page 186*): 1 tbsp
D'Anjou Pear Vinegar (*see page 184*): 2 tsp
Fee Bros Non-alcoholic Aromatic Bitters (*see page 184*): 4 dashes
Ice: Cubed
Garnish (optional): Lemon Peel
Glass: Coupe

METHOD

—

Add ingredients to a mixing glass & stir

Strain into a coupe glass

Garnish with a lemon peel (optional)

PAIS DE LA CANELA

SPICE 94 · CELERY · CINNAMON · GRAPEFRUIT

—

AIDAN BOWIE – THE AVIARY, CHICAGO

41st Best Bar in the World – World's 50 Best Bar Awards 2017

INGREDIENTS
—

Spice 94: 40ml
Celery Root & Cinnamon Cordial (*see page 65*): 20ml
Cider Spice Noir Tea: 2 tbsp
Apple Cider Vinegar: 2 dashes
Ice: Block
Garnish: Grapefruit Zest
Glass: Tumbler

METHOD
—

Add all the ingredients to a mixing glass & stir

Strain over a rock of ice into a tumbler

Garnish with grapefruit zest

BREEZE FIELD
SPICE 94 · ORANGE · PROVENCE · SAFFRON
—

GIACOMO GIANNOTTI – PARADISO, BARCELONA

36ᵗʰ Best Bar in the World – World's 50 Best Bar Awards 2017

INGREDIENTS
—

Spice 94: 50ml

Rectified Orange Juice (*see page 66*): 20ml

Bitter Orange Marmalade: 1 bar spoon

Bitter Syrup (*see page 184*): 1 tsp

Lemon & Ginger Juice (*see page 185*): 1 tbsp

Saffron Essence: 1 dash

Ice: Cubed

Garnish: Orange Twist & Lemon Thyme

Glass: Champagne Flute

METHOD
—

Add the ice & ingredients to a shaker & shake

Strain into a Champagne flute

Garnish with an orange twist & a sprig of lemon thyme

WINTER SHANDY
SPICE 94 · APRICOT · LEMON · MALT · NUTMEG

—

JOSH HARRIS – TRICK DOG, SAN FRANCISCO
26th Best Bar in the World – World's 50 Best Bar Awards 2017

INGREDIENTS
—
Spice 94: 50ml
Spiced Apricot Ceylon Shrub (*see page 66*): 25ml
Fresh Lemon Juice: 2 tsp
Sugar Syrup (*see page 186*): 1 bar spoon
Erdinger Non-alcoholic Beer: 100ml
Ice: Cubed
Garnish: Grapefruit Zest & Peel & Grated Nutmeg
Glass: Tumbler

METHOD
—
Add all the ingredients except
the Erdinger to a shaker

Add the ice & shake

Double strain into a tumbler

Add fresh cubes of ice & top with Erdinger

Garnish with grapefruit zest & peel,
then grate nutmeg over the top

ROOT CELLAR

SPICE 94 · CELERIAC · CELERY

—

ANYA MONTAGUE – BLUE HILL AT STONE BARNS, NEW YORK
12th Best Restaurant in the World – World's 50 Best Restaurant Awards 2018

INGREDIENTS
—

Spice 94: 45ml
Celeriac Root Tincture (*see page 66*): 1 tsp
Celeriac Syrup (*see page 66*): 1 tsp
Celery Seed Salt Solution (*see page 184*): 3 drops
Verjus (White Grape Juice): 2 tsp
Pu'erh Tea (*see page 186*): 2 tsp
Ice: Block
Garnish: Celery Leaf
Glass: Tumbler

METHOD
—

Add all the ingredients to a tumbler

Garnish with a celery leaf

TALLSTRUNT

SPICE 94 · CLOUDBERRY · PINE

—

JIMMIE HULTH – LINJE TIO, STOCKHOLM
44th Best Bar in the World – World's 50 Best Bar Awards 2017

INGREDIENTS

—

Spice 94: 60ml
Cloudberry Cordial (*see page 67*): 20ml
Pine Tree Syrup (*see page 67*): 2 tsp
Apple Cider Vinegar: 2 dashes
Ice: Cubed
Garnish: Spruce
Glass: Tumbler

METHOD

—

Add all the ingredients to a tumber filled with ice

Garnish with a spruce sprig

SOUVERIAN

SPICE 94 · VERJUS · PEACH · GINGER

—

DEVON TARBY – THE WALKER INN, LOS ANGELES
World Top 100 Bar – World's Best Bar Awards 2017

INGREDIENTS
—

Spice 94: 45ml
Verjus (White Grape Juice): 1 tbsp
Fresh Lemon Juice: 20ml
Spiced Peach Cordial (*see page 67*): 20ml
Ginger Syrup: 1 tsp
Ice: Pebble & Cubed
Garnish: Mint Leaf & Lemon Wheel
Glass: Tumbler

METHOD
—

Add the ingredients to a mixing glass with a small
amount of pebble ice & whip until the ice dissolves

Pour into a tumbler & add ice cubes

Cover with a second glass & shake

Strain into a tumbler over fresh ice

Garnish with a sprig of mint & a lemon wheel

GINGER & PUMPKIN SHRUB

MAKES 450ML

—

INGREDIENTS

Fresh Root Ginger: 150g
Pumpkin: 400g
Cider Vinegar: 250ml
Caster Sugar: 250g

METHOD

Peel & grate the ginger. Peel, deseed &
roughly chop the pumpkin. Add all the
ingredients to a Mason jar & muddle. Leave
for 24 hours in the fridge. Fine strain & bottle.
Keeps refrigerated for 1 month

NON-ALCOHOLIC
BITTER APERITIF

MAKES 500ML

—

INGREDIENTS

Fabri Bitter Syrup (*see page 184*): 144ml
Monin Bitter Syrup (*see page 184*): 144ml
Citric Tea (orange & pink grapefruit
peel soaked in boiling water for 1 hour,
then strained): 62ml
Wormwood Tea (wormwood chippings
soaked in boiling water for
1 hour, then strained): 75ml
Fruit Tea (Chamomile Tea, Vanilla
Black Tea, Bouquet Garni Tea &
Ground Mixed Spice soaked in boiling
water for 1 hour, then strained): 75ml

METHOD

Add all the ingredients together
& stir well. Store in glass bottles.
Keeps for 1 month

NON-ALCOHOLIC SWEET
VERMOUTH

MAKES APPROX. 1 LITRE

—

INGREDIENTS

Verjus (White Grape Juice): 480ml
Sweet & Dandy (*see page 186*): 250ml
Sorrel Juice (*see page 186*) 240ml
Tonka Bean Droplets (*see page 187*): 38
Oak Smoke Droplets (*see page 185*): 38
Vanilla Extract: 1 tsp
Caramel Syrup: 31ml
Tartaric Acid (*see page 186*): 1 tsp
Pink Grapefruit Peel: 1–2
Orange Peel: 1–2

METHOD

Add all the ingredients to a
container & stir well. Refrigerate
for 5 hours. Fine strain & bottle.
Keeps refrigerated for 3 weeks

KOLA NUT TEA

MAKES APPROX. 400ML

—

INGREDIENTS

Water: 300ml
Powdered Kola Nut (*see page 186*): 25g
Cane Sugar: 300g

METHOD

Add the water & kola nut to a saucepan
& bring to a boil. Remove from the heat
& add the sugar, stirring to dissolve.
Cover & leave for 20 minutes.
Fine strain & bottle.
Keeps for 1 month

RECTIFIED WATERMELON JUICE

MAKES 500ML

—

INGREDIENTS

Watermelon Juice: 500ml
Citric Acid: 25g
Malic Acid: 1 tbsp
Salt: Pinch

METHOD

Fine strain the watermelon juice into a bowl. Add all the other ingredients & stir, then bottle.
Keeps refrigerated for 1 week

CELERY ROOT & CINNAMON CORDIAL

MAKES APPROX. 400ML

—

INGREDIENTS

Celery Stick: 1
Salt: Pinch
Cinnamon Sticks: 25g
Caster Sugar: 250g

METHOD

Cut the celery into chunks & put through a juicer. Measure 500ml of the celery juice into a saucepan over a medium heat & reduce by half. Add the salt & stir. Remove from the heat, add the cinnamon & sugar & stir to dissolve. Leave to cool. Strain & bottle.
Keeps refrigerated for 3 weeks

MAPLE FAUX VERMOUTH

MAKES 3.75 LITRES

—

INGREDIENTS

Water: 10 litres
Grapefruit: 2
Lemons: 3
Anise Seeds: 2
Coriander Seeds: 1 tsp
Pink Peppercorns: 1 tsp
Dried Lemongrass: 1 tsp
Dried Osmanthus Flower: 2 tsp
Dried Honeysuckle: 1 tsp
Gentian: ½ tsp
Wormwood: ½ tsp
Dried Fir Tips: 2 tsp
Maple Syrup: 210ml

METHOD

Put the water into a saucepan & bring to a boil. Zest the grapefruits & lemons & add to the pan with all the other ingredients, except the maple syrup. Reduce the heat & simmer until the liquid has reduced to 3.5 litres. Strain, add the maple syrup to sweeten & bottle.
Keeps refrigerated for 2 weeks

RECTIFIED ORANGE JUICE
MAKES APPROX. 1 LITRE

—

INGREDIENTS
Fresh Orange Juice: 1 litre
Olive Oil: 40ml
Herbes de Provence: 100g

METHOD
Mix all the ingredients together
& leave to rest for 60 minutes.
Fine strain & bottle.
Keeps refrigerated for 1 week

SPICED APRICOT
CEYLON SHRUB
MAKES APPROX. 1 LITRE

—

INGREDIENTS
Green Cardamom Pods: 5
Ceylon Tea: 300ml (3 tea bags
brewed for 10 minutes, then strained)
Dried Apricots: 120g
Caster Sugar: 600g
Black Pepper: 4g
Salt: ½ tsp
Sherry Vinegar: 150ml

METHOD
Place the cardamom pods in a pan
& dry fry over a medium heat until
toasted & tinged brown. Transfer to a
large saucepan & add the tea, apricots,
sugar, pepper & salt & bring to a boil.
Remove from the heat & leave
to cool. Add the vinegar & stir.
Strain & bottle.
Keeps refrigerated for 1 month

CELERIAC ROOT TINCTURE
MAKES APPROX. 400ML

—

INGREDIENTS
Dehydrated Celeriac Peel
Dried Angelica: ½ tsp
Vegetable Glycerine (*see page 187*)

METHOD
Fill a 500ml Kilner jar ⅔ full with
celeriac peel. Add the angelica.
Top up with vegetable glycerine.
Rest in 700ml water with a circulator
(*see page 184*) for at least 24 hours.
Cool & fine strain into a bottle.
Keeps for 6 months

CELERIAC SYRUP
MAKES 500ML

—

INGREDIENTS
Water: 500ml
Sugar: 500ml
Celeriac Scraps: 250g

METHOD
Add all the ingredients to a saucepan
over a medium heat & bring to a boil.
Reduce the heat, cover with a
lid & simmer for 30 minutes.
Cool & strain into bottles.
Keeps for 1 month

CLOUDBERRY CORDIAL

MAKES APPROX. 750ML

INGREDIENTS

Honey: 500ml
Hot Water: 500ml
Cloudberries: 250g

METHOD

Add the honey to the water in a
large bowl & stir to dissolve. Add
the cloudberries & press them gently
to squeeze out the colour. Leave
for 24 hours. Strain & bottle.
(The cloudberries can be eaten
over vanilla ice cream!)
Keeps for 3 months

PINE TREE SYRUP

MAKES 750ML

INGREDIENTS

Pine Tree Needles: 500g
Caster Sugar: 500g
Water: 500ml

METHOD

Add the pine needles to the sugar
& water in a bowl & stir until the sugar
has dissolved. Vaccum pack & sous vide
(*see page 186*) for 60 minutes at 90°C.
Leave to cool. Strain & bottle.
Keeps refrigerated for 1 month

PINEAPPLE TEPACHE

MAKES APPROX. 1 LITRE

INGREDIENTS

Pineapple: 1
Sugar: 125g
Filtered Water: 1 litre

METHOD

Peel, core & chop the pineapple & add to a
Mason jar with the sugar & water & muddle.
Leave for 4 days at room temperature.
Fine strain & bottle.
Keeps refrigerated for 2 weeks

SPICED PEACH CORDIAL

MAKES APPROX. 750ML

INGREDIENTS

Fresh Root Ginger: 10g
Freshly Pressed Peach Juice: 500ml
Granulated White Sugar: 500g
Cinnamon Sticks: 10g
Ground Black Peppercorns: 1 tsp
Salt: Little Pinch

METHOD

Fill a basin with water & place an
immersion circulator (*see page 184*) inside set
at 57°C. Peel & thinly slice the ginger & add
to a Mason jar with all the other ingredients.
Seal the jar & place in the water. Leave for 2
hours. Carefully remove & transfer to an ice
bath until room temperature. Strain through
chinois & check for any floating particles.
Strain again through a 400 micron super
bag (*see page 186*), if needed, & bottle.
Keeps refrigerated for 1 month

PROFILE
Herbal & Floral

PLANTS
Peas
Hay
Rosemary
Thyme
Spearmint
Hops

FREE FROM
No Sugar
No Sweetener
No Allergens

SEEDLIP

GARDEN 108

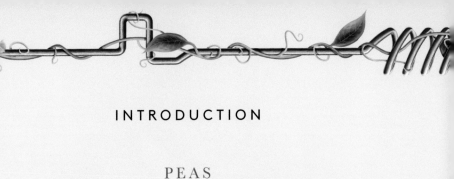

INTRODUCTION

PEAS
Pisum sativum

A delicacy in the 17th century, kings were known to
wow guests at banquets with platters of freshly picked peas.
Peas are nitrogen fixing (good for the soil) & there is more
protein in a cup of peas than in an egg, more fibre than
in a slice of wholemeal & more vitamin C than in 2 apples.
They bring all those fresh green notes to Seedlip Garden 108.
Eat your peas, please.

HAY
Lolium multiflorum

Hay is typically a blend of grasses, such as ryegrass, timothy
& brome with alfalfa & clover. Its green & dry flavours (baking
vegetables in hay is a must!) are unique to the specific blend we
use – an excellent ryegrass hay grown on our farm each year.

ROSEMARY
Rosmarinus officinalis

A woody, perennial herb with fragrant leaves native to the
Mediterranean region, rosemary brings a really herbaceous
character to the Garden 108 blend. The name derives from
the Latin for dew (*ros*) & sea (*marinus*) – 'Dew of the Sea'.

THYME
Thymus vulgaris

An aromatic perennial evergreen herb with culinary,
medicinal & ornamental uses, thyme is piney & peppery
on the palate with mint & bitter lemon notes. It is easy
to grow at home & loves well-drained soil & full sun.

SPEARMINT
Mentha spicata

The name derives from its pointed leaf tips & this
perennial herb is almost too easy to grow at home – it has
a habit of taking over! Spearmint brings the bright,
menthol freshness to the top notes of Garden 108.

HOPS
Humulus lupulus

The first documented cultivation of hops was in AD 736
in Germany & in 1524 the first British hops were grown.
Most commonly used in beer, hops bring slightly bitter
green & peppery notes to our blend.

MENU

LONG COCKTAILS
—

PEAS & LOVE
THYME
ORCHARD SPRITZ
GARDEN BOOCH
GRASS IS GREENER
MR McGREGOR
GARDEN SPRITZ

SHORT COCKTAILS
—

GARDEN SOUR
LIME
SAGE
CUCUMBER
WATERMELON

GARDEN 108
LONG COCKTAILS · SHORT COCKTAILS

CHAPTER
3

PEAS & LOVE

GARDEN 108 · TONIC/SODA · SUGAR SNAP

—

The first sugar snap pea was cultivated by Dr Calvin Lamborn in 1979
as a cross between a rogue garden pea & a mange tout.

INGREDIENTS

—

Garden 108: 50ml
Tonic/Soda: Top
Ice: Cubed
Garnish: Sugar Snap Pea
Glass: Tall

METHOD

—

Fill a tall glass with ice

Add Garden 108

Top with tonic or soda

Garnish with a gently snapped sugar snap pea

THYME

GARDEN 108 · HERBS · TONIC · LEMON THYME

—

In the 18th century thyme was recommended as a hangover cure.

INGREDIENTS

—

Garden 108: 50ml
Fever-Tree Mediterrean Tonic: Top
Ice: Cubed
Garnish: Lemon Thyme
Glass: Tall

METHOD

—

Fill a tall glass with ice

Add Garden 108

Top with tonic

Garnish with a sprig of lemon thyme

ORCHARD SPRITZ

GARDEN 108 · APPLE · PEAR · BUBBLES

—

Granny Smith apples were named after Maria Ann Smith
who first cultivated them in Australia in 1868.

INGREDIENTS

—

Garden 108: 50ml
Quality Non-alcoholic Sparkling Wine: 1 tbsp
Orchard Cordial (*see page 118*): 1 tbsp
Soda: Top
Ice: Cubed
Garnish: Apple Blossom or 3 Slices of Green Apple
Glass: Wine

METHOD

—

Fill a wine glass with ice

Add the Garden 108, sparkling wine
& Orchard Cordial & stir gently

Top with soda

Garnish with apple blossom
or 3 slices of green apple

GARDEN BOOCH

GARDEN 108 · KOMBUCHA · MINT

—

*Mint derives its name from the ancient Greek
mythical character Minthe, a river nymph.*

INGREDIENTS

—

Garden 108: 50ml
Lemongrass Kombucha (*see page 185*): Top
Ice: Cubed
Garnish: Mint
Glass: Tumbler

METHOD

—

Fill a tumbler with ice

Add Garden 108

Top with Lemongrass Kombucha

Garnish with a sprig of mint

GRASS IS GREENER

GARDEN 108 · MEADOW · GRASS · CUCUMBER FLOWER

—

*Wimbledon's grass tennis courts are thought
to be the most expensive lawns in the world.*

INGREDIENTS

—

Garden 108: 50ml
Meadow Syrup (*see page 118*): 20ml
Cut Grass Glyncture (*see page 118*): 3 drops
Soda: Top
Ice: Block
Garnish: Cucumber Flower
Glass: Tumbler

METHOD

—

Add the Garden 108, Meadow Syrup &
Cut Grass Glyncture to a tumbler over ice

Top with soda

Garnish with a cucumber flower

MR MCGREGOR

GARDEN 108 · SUGAR SNAP · CUCUMBER · CARROT

—

Until the 17th century, the only edible carrots were black, white, red & purple. Orange carrots were created by selective breeding in the Netherlands as a tribute to the ruling House of Orange.

INGREDIENTS

—

Garden 108: 50ml
Sugar Snap Shrub (*see page 118*): 20ml
Cucumber Soda: Top
Ice: Cubed
Garnish: Carrot Slice
Glass: Tall

METHOD

—

Fill a tall glass with ice

Add the Garden 108 & Sugar Snap Shrub

Top with cucumber soda

Garnish with a sliced carrot

GARDEN SPRITZ

GARDEN 108 · VERJUS · ELDERFLOWER · CELERY

—

Elderflowers have 5 petals.

INGREDIENTS
—

Garden 108: 50ml
Verjus (White Grape Juice): 20ml
Elderflower Cordial: 1 tbsp
Celery Droplets (*see page 184*): 3 drops
Soda: Top
Ice: Cubed
Garnish: Borage Flowers & Pea Tendrils
Glass: Wine

METHOD
—

Add ice to a wine glass

Add the Garden 108, verjus, elderflower
cordial & celery droplets

Top with soda

Garnish with borage flowers & pea tendrils

GARDEN SOUR

GARDEN 108 · APPLE · LEMON · ROSEMARY · THYME

—

*The number 108 refers to the average number of days
it takes to sow, grow & hand-harvest our peas.*

INGREDIENTS

—

Garden 108: 50ml
Cloudy Apple Juice: 35ml
Fresh Lemon Juice: 1 tbsp
Cider Vinegar: 1 tsp
Rosemary Sprig: 1
Thyme Sprig: 1
Sugar Syrup (*see page 186*): 2 tsp
Egg White: 1
Ice: Cubed
Garnish: Rosemary
Glass: Coupe

METHOD

—

Add all the ingredients to a shaker with ice & shake

Double strain into a coupe glass

Garnish with a rosemary sprig

LIME

GARDEN 108 · LIME · CUCUMBER

—

Limes are 88% water, 10% carbohydrates
& less than 1% each of fat & protein.

INGREDIENTS

—

Garden 108: 50ml
Sugar Syrup (*see page 186*): 2 tbsp
Fresh Lime Juice: 2 tsp
Ice: Cubed
Garnish: Cucumber Ribbon
Glass: Coupe

METHOD

—

Add all the ingredients to a shaker with ice & shake

Strain into a coupe glass

Garnish with a cucumber ribbon

SAGE

GARDEN 108 · VERJUS · SAGE

—

There are more than 900 species of sage around the world.

INGREDIENTS

—

Garden 108: 60ml
Endothermic Verjus (*see page 119*): 20ml
Nettle & Pear Shrub (*see page 119*): 2 tsp
Sage Glyncture (*see page 119*): 3 drops
Ice: Cubed
Garnish: Nasturtium Leaf
Glass: Coupe

METHOD

—

Add a scoop of ice to a mixing glass

Add all the other ingredients & stir for 30 seconds

Strain into a coupe glass

Garnish with a nasturtium leaf

GARDEN 108 · SHORT COCKTAILS
92

CUCUMBER

—

There can be a 20°C difference between the inside of a cucumber & the actual temperature outside (hence the phrase 'as cool as a cucumber').

INGREDIENTS
—

Garden 108: 60ml
Cucumber & Lemon Shrub (*see page 119*): 20ml
Salt: Pinch
Ice: Cubed
Garnish: Lemon Thyme
Glass: Coupe

METHOD
—

Add all the ingredients to a mixing glass with ice & stir

Strain into a coupe glass

Garnish with a sprig of lemon thyme

WATERMELON

GARDEN 108 · WATERMELON · BASIL

—

*Japanese farmers have been growing cube-shaped
watermelons for over 40 years!*

INGREDIENTS
—
Garden 108: 50ml
Watermelon & Basil Shrub (*see page 120*): 35ml
Egg White/Aquafaba (*see page 184*): 1 tbsp
Ice: Cubed
Garnish: Basil Leaf
Glass: Coupe

METHOD
—
Add all the ingredients except the ice to a shaker & dry shake

Add the ice & shake again

Double strain into a coupe glass

Garnish with a basil leaf

MENU

TEALIP

GARDEN COLLINS

ISLANDS IN THE STREAM #1970

PEAS & FLOWERS

IN-A-GADDA-DA-VIDA

TUFFNUT'S TONIC

SNAP!

BARBARELLESS

GOIN' BUSH

GARDEN 108

GUEST COCKTAILS

A selection of cocktails from some of the world's best bartenders

CHAPTER

4

TEALIP
GARDEN 108 · BERGAMOT · G&TEA
—

XAV LANDAIS – SEXY FISH, LONDON
Bar with the largest Japanese whisky collection in Europe

INGREDIENTS
—
Garden 108: 30ml
Bergamot Purée: 2 tbsp
G&Tea Cordial (*see page 120*): 2 tbsp
Ice: Block
Garnish: None
Glass: Teacup

METHOD
—
Add all the ingredients to a mixing glass & shake

Fine strain into a teacup over an ice block

GARDEN COLLINS

GARDEN 108 · APPLE · ELDERFLOWER · CUCUMBER · BASIL

—

JACK MCGARRY – THE DEAD RABBIT & BLACKTAIL, NEW YORK CITY

5th & 32nd Best Bars in the World – World's 50 Best Bar Awards 2017

INGREDIENTS

—

Garden 108: 50ml
Fresh Lemon Juice: 20ml
Freshly Pressed Granny Smith Apple Juice: 20ml
Elderflower Lemon Sherbet (*see page 120*): 2 tbsp
Cucumber Soda: Top
Ice: Cubed
Garnish: Basil Leaf
Glass: Tall

METHOD

—

Add the Garden 108, lemon juice,
apple juice & Elderflower Lemon Sherbet
to a shaker with ice & shake

Strain into a tall glass over ice

Top with cucumber soda

Garnish with a basil leaf

ISLANDS IN THE STREAM #1970

GARDEN 108 · PINK GRAPEFRUIT · MANGOSTEEN

—

AGUNG PRABOWO – THE OLD MAN BAR, HONG KONG

5ᵗʰ Best Bar in Asia – Asia's 50 Best Bar Awards 2018

INGREDIENTS
—

Garden 108: 375ml
Clarified Pink Grapefruit Juice (*see page 121*): 600ml
Clear Mangosteen Juice (*see page 121*): 50ml
Water: 75ml
Sugar Syrup (*see page 186*): 87.5ml
Salt: 2 pinches
Ice: Cubed
Garnish: Grapefruit Zest & Mangosteen Wheel
Glass: Tall

METHOD
—

Add all the ingredients to a Twist & Sparkle bottle
(these are used by bartenders to carbonate drinks)

Pour into 4 tall glasses over ice

Garnish with grapefruit zest & a mangosteen wheel

PEAS & FLOWERS

GARDEN 108 · HONEY · LEMON BALM · PEA TENDRILS

—

LUKE WHEARTY – OPERATION DAGGER, SINGAPORE

24th Best Bar in the World – World's 50 Best Bar Awards 2017

INGREDIENTS
—

Garden 108: 50ml
Honey Syrup (*see page 185*): 25ml
Lemon Balm Vinegar (*see page 121*): 20ml
Soda: Top
Ice: Cubed
Garnish: Pea Tendrils & Seasonal Edible Flowers (if available)
Glass: Tall

METHOD
—

Fill a tall glass with ice

Add the Garden 108, honey syrup & Lemon Balm Vinegar

Top with soda

Garnish with pea tendrils & seasonal edible flowers

IN-A-GADDA-DA-VIDA

GARDEN 108 · PUFF PASTRY · PEAR · KAFFIR LIME

—

CHRIS HYSTED-ADAMS — BLACK PEARL, MELBOURNE
22nd Best Bar in the World — World's 50 Best Bar Awards 2017

INGREDIENTS
—

Garden 108: 30ml
Fresh Lime Juice: 20ml
Pear & Kaffir Lime Syrup (*see page 121*): 25ml
Puff Pastry Cream (*see page 122*): 2 tbsp
Egg White: 1
Mineral Water: 60ml
Ice: Crushed
Garnish: Kaffir Lime Leaf Disc
Glass: Chilled Tall

METHOD
—

Spindle mix (*see page 186*) the Garden 108,
lime juice, Pear & Kaffir Syrup,
Puff Pastry Cream & egg white in a mixing
glass with a small handful of crushed ice

When the ice has dissolved, pour the
mineral water into a chilled tall glass

Top with the mixed ingredients

Garnish with a kaffir lime leaf disc

TUFFNUT'S TONIC

GARDEN 108 · CUCUMBER · SHISO · DRAGON EYE

—

JIM MEEHAN – PDT, NEW YORK & HONG KONG

World Top 100 Bar – World's Best Bar Awards 2017

INGREDIENTS

—

Garden 108: 50ml

Cucumber Wheels: 2

Shiso Leaf (*see page 186*): 1

Dragon Fruit Syrup (*see page 123*): 2 tsp

Fresh Lime Juice: 1 tbsp

East Imperial Tonic: 50ml

Ice: Cubed

Garnish: Shiso Leaf

Glass: Tall

METHOD

—

Muddle the cucumber wheels & shiso leaf in a shaker
with the Dragon Fruit Syrup

Add the Garden 108 & lime juice & shake

Add the tonic then fine strain into a tall glass filled with ice

Garnish with a shiso leaf

SNAP!

—

ALEX KRATENA – EX BAR MANAGER OF ARTESIAN, LONDON
& CO-FOUNDER OF (P)OUR

INGREDIENTS
—

Garden 108: 40ml
Buttermilk Vinaigrette (*see page 123*): 40ml
Sugar Snap Pea Syrup (*see page 123*): 1 tbsp
Timut Pepper (*see page 187*): 1 pinch
Ice: Cubed
Garnish: 3 Timut Peppercorns
Glass: Chilled Coupe

METHOD
—

Add all the ingredients to a shaker with ice & shake

Strain into a chilled coupe glass

Garnish with 3 timut peppercorns

BARBARELLESS

—

TESS POSTHUMUS – THE FLYING DUTCHMEN, AMSTERDAM

Top 10 International Bartender of the Year 2017, Tales of the Cocktail

INGREDIENTS
—

Garden 108: 45ml
Fresh Lime Juice: 20ml
Grapefruit & Chilli Syrup (*see page 123*): 1 tbsp
Salt: Pinch
Rhubarb Soda (*see page 186*): Top
Ice: Cubed
Garnish: Rhubarb Ribbon
Glass: Tall

METHOD
—

Add the Garden 108, lime juice, Grapefruit
& Chilli Syrup & salt to a shaker & shake

Strain into a tall glass filled with ice

Top with rhubarb soda

Garnish with a rhubarb ribbon

GOIN' BUSH

GARDEN 108 · AVOCADO · EUCALYPTUS · GRAPE

———

IAIN GRIFFITHS – TRASH TIKI, SUPER LYAN & DANDELYAN

Dandelyan 2nd Best Bar in the World – World's 50 Best Bar Awards 2017

INGREDIENTS
———

Garden 108: 30ml
Avocado Pit Honey (*see page 122*): 2 tsp
Fresh Grapefruit Juice: 1 tsp
Pea & Eucalyptus Soda (*see page 122*): Top
Ice: Cubed
Garnish: Compressed White Grape (*see page 122*)
Glass: Tall

METHOD
———

Add all the ingredients to a tall glass

Garnish with a compressed white grape

ORCHARD CORDIAL
MAKES APPROX. 600ML

—

INGREDIENTS
Caster Sugar: 400g
Apple Juice: 200ml
Pear Juice: 200ml

METHOD
Add all the ingredients to a saucepan
& bring to a boil. Reduce the heat, cover
& simmer for 30 minutes. Leave to cool,
then strain into a bottle.
Keeps for 1 month

MEADOW SYRUP
MAKES 375ML

—

INGREDIENTS
Meadowsweet: Handful
Sorrel: Handful
Honeysuckle: Handful
Water: 250ml
Sugar: 250g
Malic Acid: 1 tsp

METHOD
Vacuum pack & sous vide (*see page 186*)
all the ingredients together for
60 minutes at 75°C.
Cool & strain into a bottle.
Keeps for 1 week

CUT GRASS GLYNCTURE
MAKES 350ML

—

INGREDIENTS
Freshly Cut & Washed Grass
Water: 100ml
Vegetable Glycerine (*see page 187*): 250ml

METHOD
Fill a 500ml Mason jar ⅔ full with grass.
Add the water & vegetable glycerine
& seal. Refrigerate for 3 days.
Fine strain & bottle.
Keeps for 6 months

SUGAR SNAP
SHRUB
MAKES 250ML

—

INGREDIENTS
Sugar Snap Peas: 250g
Apple Cider Vinegar: 250ml
Caster Sugar: 250g

METHOD
Finely slice the peas & place in a
Mason jar with the other ingredients.
Muddle hard then leave overnight.
Strain & bottle.
Keeps refrigerated for 2 weeks

ENDOTHERMIC VERJUS

MAKES 250ML

—

INGREDIENTS

Sansho Peppercorns: 15
Verjus (White Grape Juice): 250ml

METHOD

Use a pestle & mortar to break open
the peppercorns. Add to a Mason jar
with the verjus & mix. Leave in the fridge
for 2 hours. Fine strain & bottle.
Keeps refrigerated for 2 weeks

NETTLE & PEAR SHRUB

MAKES 400ML

—

INGREDIENTS

Nettles: 100g
Sliced Pears: 3
Apple Cider Vinegar: 250ml
Caster Sugar: 250g

METHOD

Add the nettles & pears to a
Mason jar & muddle. Add the vinegar
& sugar & stir. Leave for 24 hours.
Fine strain & bottle.
Keeps refrigerated for 1 month

SAGE GLYNCTURE

MAKES 275ML

—

INGREDIENTS

Sage Leaves: 3 handfuls
Vegetable Glycerine (*see page 187*): 200ml
Water: 75ml

METHOD

Fill a 500ml Mason jar ⅔ full with
sage leaves. Cover with the vegetable
glycerin & water. Leave for 48 hours.
Fine strain & bottle.
Keeps for 6 months

CUCUMBER & LEMON SHRUB

MAKES 400ML

—

INGREDIENTS

Lemons: 3
Finely Sliced Cucumbers: 3
Apple Cider Vinegar: 200ml
Caster Sugar: 200g

METHOD

Remove the peel from the lemons &
add to a Mason jar with the cucumbers
& muddle. Add the vinegar & sugar
& stir. Refrigerate for 24 hours.
Fine strain & bottle.
Keeps for 1 week

WATERMELON & BASIL SHRUB
MAKES 400ML

—

INGREDIENTS
Watermelon: ½
Basil: Handful
Apple Cider Vinegar: 200ml
Sugar: 200g

METHOD
Chop the watermelon flesh & add to a
Mason jar with the basil leaves & muddle.
Add the vinegar & sugar & shake. Leave
for 24 hours. Fine strain & bottle.
Keeps refrigerated for 1 month

BLUEBERRY SHRUB
MAKES APPROX. 750ML

—

INGREDIENTS
Fresh Blueberries: 560g
Cider Vinegar: 280ml
Caster Sugar: 280g
Garnish: Skewers of blueberries
(optional)

METHOD
Place the blueberries in a nonmetallic
container & add the vinegar. Cover
tightly & refrigerate for at least 3 days.
Pour through a sieve & press the berries
to release their juices. Pour the blueberry
liquid into a medium saucepan, add the
sugar & boil for 3 minutes, stirring
occasionally. Remove from the heat
& leave to cool. Bottle & chill.
Keeps refrigerated for 1 month

G&TEA CORDIAL
MAKES 1.25 LITRES

—

INGREDIENTS
G&Tea flavoured tea bags
[Fortnum & Mason]: 6
Boiling Water: 800ml
Sugar: 800g

METHOD
Steep the tea bags in the water for
10 minutes. Strain & add the sugar.
Leave to cool.
Keeps for 1 month

ELDERFLOWER LEMON SHERBET
MAKES 1 LITRE

—

INGREDIENTS
Lemons: 6
Sugar: 750g
Fresh Lemon Juice: 375ml
Elderflower Tea (cold infusion): 375ml

METHOD
Remove the zest from the lemons & add
to a bowl with the sugar. Mix thoroughly
so the oils from the zest begin to express
into the sugar. Leave at room temperature
for at least 1 hour (or vacuum pack
the zest & sugar for faster results – *see page
187*). Tip the mixture into a saucepan &
add the lemon juice & tea. Place over a
medium heat & cook at 60°C, stirring
regularly, for 30 minutes, until the sugar
has completely dissolved. Pour through
a fine mesh strainer & bottle.
Keeps refrigerated for 1 month

CLARIFIED PINK GRAPEFRUIT JUICE
MAKES 1 LITRE

—

INGREDIENTS

Grapefruit Juice: 1 litre
Pectinex Ultra SP-L (*see page 186*): 2g
Chitosan (*see page 184*): 2g
Kieselsol (*see page 183*): 2g

METHOD

Add the ingredients to a centrifuge
(*see page 184*) & spin for 5 minutes
at high speed. Place the clarified juice
into a separate container.
Keeps refrigerated for 1 week

CLEAR MANGOSTEEN JUICE
MAKES 1 LITRE

—

INGREDIENTS

Mangosteen: 1.5kg
Caster Sugar: 500g
Water: 500ml
Pectinex Ultra SP-L (*see page 186*): 1 tsp

METHOD

Remove the mangosteen pulp & place
in a blender with the other ingredients
in a heavy-duty blender. Blend until the
sugar has dissolved. Place half the
mixture in a centrifuge (*see page 184*)
& spin at the highest speed (4000 rpm)
for 25 minutes. Strain through a
cheesecloth into a bottle. Repeat with
the second half of the mixture.
Keeps refrigerated for 1 week

LEMON BALM VINEGAR
MAKES 1 LITRE

—

INGREDIENTS

Lemon Pelargonium Leaves
(*see page 185*): 50g
Apple Cider Vinegar: 1 litre

METHOD

Add both the ingredients to a saucepan
& bring to a boil. Boil for 3 minutes.
Remove from the heat & leave to cool.
Strain & bottle.
Keeps refrigerated for 1 month

PEAR & KAFFIR LIME SYRUP
MAKES APPROX. 250ML

—

INGREDIENTS

Nashi Pears: 3
Caster Sugar: about 250g
Large Kaffir Lime Leaves: 2

METHOD

Juice the pears & measure the liquid.
Pour into a saucepan & add the same
weight of sugar. Add the kaffir lime
leaves & heat very gently, stirring until
the sugar has dissolved. Remove from the
heat & steep for 1 hour. Strain & bottle.
Keeps for 1 month

PUFF PASTRY CREAM
MAKES 500ML

—

INGREDIENTS
Puff Pastry Sheets: 2
Double Cream: 500ml

METHOD
Preheat the oven to 170°C.
Place the sheets of puff pastry between
2 baking trays. Bake until golden brown
& crisp. Break into smaller pieces &
submerge in the cream in a non-reactive
bowl. Cover with cling film & refrigerate
overnight. Strain, making sure to
squeeze all the infused cream from
any lumps of pastry. Bottle.
Keeps refrigerated for 1 week

PEA & EUCALYPTUS SODA
MAKES 750ML

—

INGREDIENTS
Freeze-dried Peas: ½ tsp
Dried Eucalyptus: Pinch
Boiling Water: 750ml
Malic Acid: Pinch
Caster Sugar: 1 tsp

METHOD
Blend the peas & eucalyptus in a spice
grinder. Add to a bowl with the boiling
water, the malic acid & the sugar. Brew for
5 minutes, stirring constantly. Strain into
bottles. Leave to cool, then chill. Use an ISI
Soda Syphon with 1 Co2 & 1 No2 bulbs.
Keeps for 1 week

AVOCADO PIT HONEY
MAKES 1 LITRE

—

INGREDIENTS
Avocado Stones: 6
Local Honey: 750g
Boiling Water: 250ml

METHOD
Clean & dry the avocado stones.
Finely grate them, then place in a dry
pan. Toast over a medium heat until
pinkish-red. Remove from the heat & tip
into a bowl with the honey & boiling
water. Leave to rest for 1 day.
Strain & store in jars.
Keeps for 6 months

COMPRESSED WHITE GRAPES
MAKES 250G

—

INGREDIENTS
Under-ripe White Grapes: 250g
Dried Avocado Leaf: 10g
Boiling Water: 500ml
Caster Sugar: 50g
White Wine Vinegar: 2 tsp

METHOD
De-stem the grapes & pierce them a few
times with a toothpick. Brew the avocado
leaf in the boiling water for 10 minutes.
Strain & leave to cool. Add the sugar &
vinegar to the brew & stir to dissolve the
sugar. Place in a Kilner jar with the
grapes & seal. Refrigerate for 3 days.
Keeps for 1 week

DRAGON FRUIT SYRUP
MAKES 500ML

—

INGREDIENTS
Dried Dragon Eye (Logan): 50g
Sugar Syrup (*see page 186*): 550ml

METHOD
Measure the ingredients into a saucepan
& place over a medium heat.
Simmer gently for 5 minutes.
Remove from the heat & fine strain.
Leave to cool, then bottle.
Keeps refrigerated for 1 month

BUTTERMILK VINAIGRETTE
MAKES APPROX. 1 LITRE

—

INGREDIENTS
Organic Buttermilk: 1 litre
White Balsamic Vinegar: 100ml
Extra Virgin Olive Oil: 1 tsp
Salt: Pinch

METHOD
Using an immersion blender, blend
all ingredients until fully emulsified.
Store in an airtight container.
Keeps refrigerated for 3 days

SUGAR SNAP PEA SYRUP
MAKES 800ML

—

INGREDIENTS
Sugar Snap Peas: 250g
Rich Sugar Syrup (*see page 186*): 800g

METHOD
Roughly chop the peas & place in a
non-reactive container with the syrup.
Infuse for 24 hours. Strain & place
in an airtight container.
Keeps refrigerated for 2 weeks

GRAPEFRUIT &
CHILLI SYRUP
MAKES 450ML

—

INGREDIENTS
Red Grapefruits: 3
Caster Sugar: 250g
Water: 250ml
Sliced Red Chilli: 1

METHOD
Grate the peel of the grapefruits into
a bowl. Add the sugar & stir vigorously.
Crush the peels into the sugar until
slushy. Cover & leave overnight.
Place the water in a saucepan & bring
to a boil. Stir in the citrus sugar & add
the sliced chilli. Simmer for 3 minutes
to dissolve the sugar. Remove from
the heat & leave to cool. Strain the
liquid, discarding the peel,
chilli & seeds. Bottle.
Keeps for 1 month

PROFILE

Citrus & Warm

PLANTS

Plants
Bitter Orange
Blood Orange
Mandarin
Ginger
Lemongrass
Lemon

FREE FROM

No Sugar
No Sweetener
No Allergens

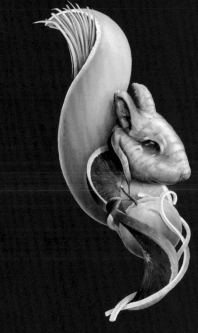

SEEDLIP

—

GROVE 42

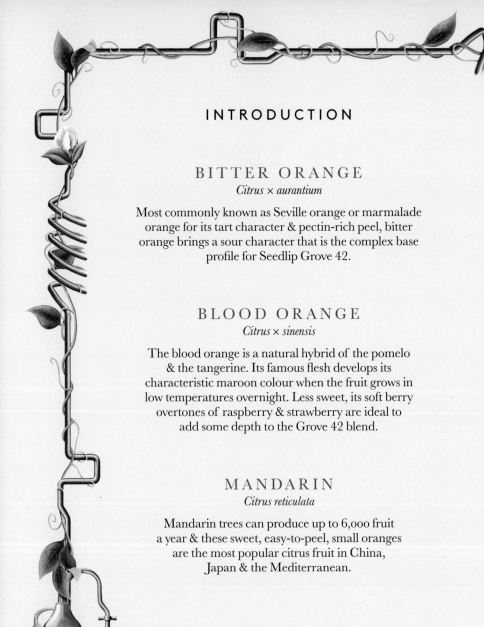

INTRODUCTION

BITTER ORANGE
Citrus × aurantium

Most commonly known as Seville orange or marmalade orange for its tart character & pectin-rich peel, bitter orange brings a sour character that is the complex base profile for Seedlip Grove 42.

BLOOD ORANGE
Citrus × sinensis

The blood orange is a natural hybrid of the pomelo & the tangerine. Its famous flesh develops its characteristic maroon colour when the fruit grows in low temperatures overnight. Less sweet, its soft berry overtones of raspberry & strawberry are ideal to add some depth to the Grove 42 blend.

MANDARIN
Citrus reticulata

Mandarin trees can produce up to 6,000 fruit a year & these sweet, easy-to-peel, small oranges are the most popular citrus fruit in China, Japan & the Mediterranean.

GINGER
Zingiber officinale

The ginger plant is a herbaceous perennial that grows
about a metre tall & is from the same family as tumeric,
cardamom & galangal. Its root adds a sweet warmth
to the Grove 42 blend.

LEMONGRASS
Cymbopogon citratus

Also known as barbed wire grass or silky heads,
lemongrass is a tropical island plant of the grass family
& is widely used in medicine & cooking. It brings
a perfect balance between complex rooty spice
& zesty freshness to Grove 42.

LEMON
Citrus × limon

Lemons are actually a hybrid of a sour orange
& a citron, & the world grows approximately
16 million tonnes of them every year!

MENU

LONG COCKTAILS

NOTHING RHYMES WITH ORANGE

PEEL

MALT

THOROUGHBRED

WOOD

CLEMENTS

CASCARA

CITRUS

SHORT COCKTAILS

MANGO

BLOSSOM

MILK PUNCH

HONEY

CASHEW PUNCH

GROVE 42
LONG COCKTAILS · SHORT COCKTAILS

CHAPTER
5

NOTHING RHYMES
WITH ORANGE

—

*The Number 42 refers to 1542, the year the word orange
was first used to describe a colour.*

INGREDIENTS

—

Grove 42: 50ml
Soda/Tonic: Top
Ice: Cubed
Garnish: Orange Twist
Glass: Tall

METHOD

—

Fill a tall glass with ice

Add Grove 42

Top with soda or tonic

Garnish with an orange twist

PEEL

—

There are 1.3 billion tonnes of food wasted every year.
Here's the perfect use for those unwanted carrot peelings.

INGREDIENTS

—

Grove 42: 50ml
Carrot Cordial (*see page 166*): 20ml
Soda: Top
Ice: Cubed
Garnish: Sage Leaf
Glass: Tumbler

METHOD

—

Fill a tumbler with ice

Add the Grove 42 & Carrot Cordial

Top with soda

Garnish with a sage leaf

MALT

—

*Roasted barley was used as a coffee substitute during
the First & Second World Wars in Italy.*

INGREDIENTS
—

Grove 42: 50ml
Malt Syrup (*see page 166*): 20ml
Bonfire Glyncture (*see page 166*): 2 drops
Fresh Lemon Juice: 2 tsp
Soda: Top
Ice: Cubed
Garnish: Orange Slice
Glass: Tall

METHOD
—

Fill a tall glass with ice

Add the Grove 42, Malt Syrup, Bonfire Glyncture & lemon juice

Top with soda

Garnish with an orange slice

THOROUGHBRED

GROVE 42 · GINGER · LIME

—

A male mule is called a john.

INGREDIENTS
—

Grove 42: 50ml
Ginger Beer: Top
Ice: Cubed
Garnish: Lime Wheel
Glass: Tumbler

METHOD
—

Fill a tumbler with ice

Add the Grove 42

Top with ginger beer

Garnish with a lime wheel

WOOD

GROVE 42 · CHAR · BLOOD ORANGE

—

*The blood orange was once reserved for royalty & the very privileged,
so it features in many early European paintings, mosaics & poems.*

INGREDIENTS

—

Grove 42: 50ml
Fever-Tree Smoked Ginger Ale: Top
Ice: Cubed
Garnish: Blood Orange Wheel
Glass: Tumbler

METHOD

—

Fill a tumbler with ice

Add the Grove 42

Top with the ginger ale

Garnish with a wheel of blood orange

CLEMENTS

GROVE 42 · SUNSHINE · FLOWERS

—

One million Earths could fit inside the Sun.

INGREDIENTS

—

Grove 42: 50ml
Sunshine Syrup (*see page 166*) 20ml
Soda: Top
Ice: Cubed
Garnish: Seasonal Flower
Glass: Champagne Flute

METHOD

—

Add the Grove 42, Sunshine Syrup & ice to a shaker & shake

Strain into a Champagne flute

Top with soda

Garnish with a flower

CASCARA

GROVE 42 · CASCARA · HIBISCUS

—

Cascaras are the dried skins of coffee cherries.

INGREDIENTS
—

Grove 42: 50ml
Cascara Syrup (*see page 167*): 1 tbsp
Soda: Top
Ice: Cubed
Garnish: Hibiscus Flowers
Glass: Tumbler

METHOD
—

Fill a tumbler with ice

Add the Grove 42 & Cascara Syrup

Top with soda

Garnish with hibiscus flowers

CITRUS

GROVE 42 · BUBBLES · CITRUS

—

Joseph Priestly invented carbonated water in 1767.

INGREDIENTS

—

Grove 42: 50ml
Sugar-free Lemon & Lime Soda: Top
Ice: Cubed
Garnish: Blood Orange Slice
Glass: Tall

METHOD

—

Fill a tall glass with ice

Add Grove 42

Top with soda

Garnish with a blood orange slice

MANGO

GROVE 42 · YUZU · MANGO

—

More fresh mangoes are eaten around the world
each day than any other fruit

INGREDIENTS

—

Grove 42: 50ml
Yuzu Verjus (*see page 167*): 20ml
Mango Drops (*see page 167*): 3
Ice: Cubed
Garnish (optional): Orange Twist
Glass: Coupe

METHOD

—

Add all the ingredients to a mixing glass
filled with ice & stir for 30 seconds

Strain into a coupe glass

Garnish with an orange twist (optional)

BLOSSOM

—

June 27th is National Orange Blossom Day in the USA.

INGREDIENTS

—

Grove 42: 50ml
Fresh Orange Juice: 35ml
Fresh Lemon Juice: 2 tsp
Cider Vinegar: 1 tsp
Lemongrass Stalk: 1
Sugar Syrup (*see page 186*): 1 tbsp
Orange Blossom Water (*see page 185*): 1 drop
Egg White: 1
Ice: Cubed
Garnish: Orange Leaf
Glass: Coupe

METHOD

—

Add all the ingredients to a shaker with the ice & hard shake

Double strain into a coupe glass

Garnish with an orange leaf

MILK PUNCH

GROVE 42 · ALMOND · CITRUS

—

*The first milk punch was recorded in William Sacheverell's 1688 travelogue
of the Scottish isle of Iona. This is the first non-alcoholic version!*

INGREDIENTS

—

Grove 42: 700ml
Almond Milk: 125ml
Whole Milk: 125ml
Rooibos & Turmeric Cordial (*see page 167*): 190ml
Fresh Lemon Juice: 60ml
Fresh Grapefruit Juice: 50ml
Ice: Block
Garnish: Blood Orange Peel
Glass: Tumbler

METHOD

—

Bring the almond & whole milk to a simmer over a medium heat

Pour into a large pitcher

Mix the Grove 42, cordial & juices in a separate jug

Slowly add this to the milk & allow it to curdle

Leave for 30 minutes, then strain through a coffee filter

Bottle & store for up to 1 week

Serve with ice & garnish with a blood orange twist

HONEY

GROVE 42 · NECTAR · GORSE · MANDARIN

—

Honey is the only food that humans eat that an insect produces.

INGREDIENTS
—

Grove 42: 50ml
Gorse & Bees Wax Shrub (*see page 168*): 20ml
Fresh Mandarin Juice: 25ml
Honey Droplet: 1
Ice: Cubed
Garnish: Honey Drip
Glass: Tumbler

METHOD
—

Add the ingredients to a shaker
without ice & throw several times

Add ice & shake

Double strain into a tumbler

Garnish with a drip of honey

CASHEW PUNCH

GROVE 42 · CASHEW · GINGER

—

Raw cashews are green & cashews are actually a seed & not a nut.

INGREDIENTS

—

Grove 42: 700ml
Cashew Milk: 125ml
Whole Milk: 125ml
Ginger Cordial: 90ml
Fresh Lemon Juice: 70ml
Ice: Cubed
Garnish: Candied Ginger Cube with Sugar Coating Removed
Glass: Coupe

METHOD

—

Bring the cashew & whole milk to a simmer over medium heat

Pour into a large pitcher

Mix the Grove 42, cordial & juice in a separate jug

Slowly add this to the milk & allow it to curdle

Leave for 30 minutes, then strain through a coffee filter

Bottle & store for up to 1 week

Add ice & strain into a coupe glass

Garnish with de-sugared candied ginger cube

CUCUMBER

GARDEN 108 · CUCUMBER · LEMON THYME

—

There can be a 20°C difference between the inside of a cucumber & the
actual temperature outside (hence the phrase 'as cool as a cucumber').

INGREDIENTS

—

Garden 108: 60ml
Cucumber & Lemon Shrub (*see page 119*): 20ml
Salt: Pinch
Ice: Cubed
Garnish: Lemon Thyme
Glass: Coupe

METHOD

—

Add all the ingredients to a mixing glass with ice & stir

Strain into a coupe glass

Garnish with a sprig of lemon thyme

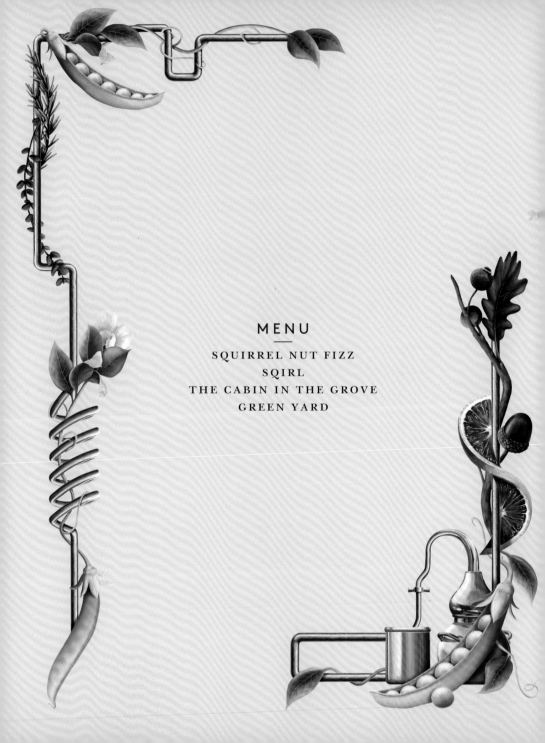

MENU

SQUIRREL NUT FIZZ
SQIRL
THE CABIN IN THE GROVE
GREEN YARD

GROVE 42

GUEST COCKTAILS

A selection of cocktails from some of the world's best bartenders

CHAPTER
6

SQUIRREL NUT FIZZ

GROVE 42 · RIBENA · VANILLA · PEANUT

—

RYAN CHETIYAWARDANA – CUB, SUPER LYAN, DANDELYAN, LONDON

Dandelyan 2ⁿᵈ Best Bar in the World – World's 50 Best Bar Awards 2017

INGREDIENTS

—

Grove 42: 55ml
Ribena: 1 tsp
Honey Syrup (*see page 185*): 2 tsp
Fresh Blood Orange Juice: 1 tbsp
Fresh Lemon Juice: 1 tbsp
Egg White: 1
Vanilla Peanut Milk (*see page 187*): 1 tsp
Chilled Soda: Top
Ice: Cubed
Garnish: Rosemary Dust (*see page 168*)
Glass: Chilled Tall

METHOD

—

Add all the ingredients except the soda
to a shaker without ice & dry shake

Add ice & shake again

Double strain into a chilled tall glass

Top with chilled soda

Garnish with rosemary dust

SQIRL

GROVE 42 · YUZU · CARDAMOM

—

MATT WHILEY – SCOUT, LONDON
World Top 100 Bar – World's Best Bar Awards 2017

INGREDIENTS
—
Grove 42: 60ml
Yuzu Juice (*see page 187*): 20ml
Cardamom Syrup (*see page 168*): 1 tbsp
Ice: 1 small scoop
Glass: Continental Beer
Garnish: Mint Leaf & Orange Disc

METHOD
—
Add all the ingredients, including the ice,
to a blender & blitz until smooth

Pour into a Continental beer glass & serve as a slushy

Garnish with a mint leaf & orange disc

THE CABIN
IN THE GROVE
GROVE 42 · PINE · PLUM · LAPSANG
—

ROB SIMPSON – THE CLOVE CLUB, LONDON
33rd Best Restaurant in the World – World's 50 Best Restaurant Awards 2018

INGREDIENTS
—
Grove 42: 50ml
Pine-smoked Blood Orange Juice (*see page 169*): 20ml
Pine Cordial (*see page 169*): 20ml
Spiced Grilled Plum Purée (*see page 169*): 1 tbsp
Cold-brewed Lapsang Souchong Tea: 1 tbsp
Salt: Pinch
Ice: Block
Garnish: Blood Orange Twist & Pine
Glass: Tumbler

METHOD
—
Add all the ingredients to a shaker & shake

Toss the mixture over ice, between the shaker, a couple of times

Strain into a tumbler & add ice

Garnish with a blood orange twist & a sprig of pine

GREEN YARD

GROVE 42 · LEMON · BASIL · MATCHA

—

ERIK LORINCZ – AMERICAN BAR AT THE SAVOY, LONDON

Best Bar in the World – World's 50 Best Bar Awards 2017

INGREDIENTS

—

Grove 42: 50ml
Fresh Lemon Juice: 2 tbsp
Sugar Syrup (*see page 186*): 1 tbsp
Basil Leaf: 1
Cardamom Droplets (*see page 184*): 3
Egg White: 1
Ice: Cubed
Garnish: Matcha Powder (*see page 185*)
Glass: Coupe

METHOD

—

Add all the ingredients, except the ice,
to a jug & blend with a hand blender

Tip into a shaker with the ice & shake

Double strain into a coupe glass

Garnish with a sprinkle of matcha powder

CARROT CORDIAL

MAKES 500ML

—

INGREDIENTS

Water: 500ml
Caster Sugar: 500g
Carrot Peelings: 250g

METHOD

Add all the ingredients to a saucepan over a medium heat & bring to a boil. Reduce the heat, cover & simmer for 30 minutes. Remove from the heat, cool & strain into a bottle.
Keeps refrigerated for 1 month

MALT SYRUP

MAKES 450ML

—

INGREDIENTS

Water: 250ml
Caster Sugar: 250g
Cacao: 20g
Toasted Unmalted Barley: 40g

METHOD

Add the water to a saucepan & bring to a boil. Add the sugar, stirring until it dissolves. Remove from the heat & leave to cool. Add the cacao & barley & stir. Leave for 30 minutes. Strain & bottle.
Keeps for 1 month

BONFIRE GLYNCTURE

MAKES 275ML

—

INGREDIENTS

Manuka Bark (*see page 185*): 10g
Lapsang Souchong Tea: 50g
Timut Pepper (*see page 187*): 30g
Vegetable Glycerine (*see page 187*): 200ml
Water: 75ml

METHOD

Mix the manuka bark, tea & pepper in a Mason jar. Add the vegetable glycerin & water & leave for 2 days. Strain & bottle.
Keeps for 6 months

SUNSHINE SYRUP

MAKES 250ML

—

INGREDIENTS

Orange: 1
Lemon: 1
Grapefruit: 1
Caster Sugar: 500g
Water: 250ml

METHOD

Zest the orange, lemon & grapefruit & add to a saucepan over a medium heat with the other ingredients & bring to a boil. Reduce the heat & simmer for 30 minutes. Strain & leave to cool. Bottle.
Keeps for 1 month

CASCARA SYRUP
MAKES 400ML

—

INGREDIENTS
Caster Sugar: 250g
Water: 250ml
Cascara (*see page 184*): 125g

METHOD
Add the sugar, water & cascara to a
saucepan over a medium heat & bring
to a boil. Stir until the sugar dissolves
Remove from the heat & leave to cool.
Strain & bottle.
Keeps refrigerated for 1 month

YUZU VERJUS
MAKES 120ML

—

INGREDIENTS
Yuzu Juice (*see page 187*): 2 tsp
Sugar Syrup (*see page 186*): 2 tsp
Verjus (White Grape Juice): 100ml

METHOD
Add the yuzu juice, sugar syrup
& verjus to a bottle & shake.
Keeps for 1 week

MANGO DROPS
MAKES 300ML

—

INGREDIENTS
Mango: 1
Vegetable Glycerine (*see page 187*):
200ml
Water: 100ml

METHOD
Dice the mango & add to a Mason jar.
Pour in the vegetable glycerine & water.
Leave for 48 hours in the fridge.
Strain & bottle.
Keeps for 1 month

ROOIBOS & TURMERIC CORDIAL
MAKES APPROX. 400ML

INGREDIENTS
Rooibos Tea: 25g
Ground Turmeric: Pinch
Caster Sugar: 500g
Hot Water: 250ml

METHOD
Add the ingredients to a bowl & stir well.
Leave to infuse until cold.
Strain & bottle.
Keeps refrigerated for 1 week

GORSE & BEESWAX SHRUB
MAKES 250ML

—

INGREDIENTS
Gorse Flowers: 250g
Beeswax: 10g
Lincolnshire Honey: 200g
Raw Apple Vinegar: 200ml

METHOD
Add all the ingredients to a bowl & mix
together. Sous vide (*see page 186*) at 52° for
6 hours. Fine strain & bottle.
Keeps refrigerated for 1 month

VANILLA PEANUT MILK
MAKES 500ML

—

INGREDIENTS
Unsalted Peanuts: 200g
Water: 400ml
Vanilla Pod: ½

METHOD
Preheat the oven to 170°C.
Place the peanuts on a baking tray &
roast until golden & smelling delicious.
Soak in water overnight (this makes them
easier to blitz). Tip the peanuts & water
into a blender. Scrape the seeds from the
vanilla pod & add to the peanuts. Blend
until smooth. Pass through a super bag
(*see page 186*), then bottle.
Keeps refrigerated for 3 days

ROSEMARY DUST
MAKES 1 TBSP

—

INGREDIENTS
Rosemary Sprig: 1
Sugar Syrup (*see page 186*): 20ml
Salt: Pinch
Matcha Powder (*see page 185*): ¼ tsp

METHOD
Dip the rosemary sprig in the sugar
syrup, then sprinkle with salt. Dehydrate
overnight in a dehydrator or in an oven
set to a low temperature. When brittle,
grind in a pestle & mortar. Sieve to get
a fine powder. Add matcha powder.
Keep in an airtight container for 6 months

CARDAMOM SYRUP
MAKES 325ML

—

INGREDIENTS
Water: 250ml
Cardamom Pods: 60g
Caster Sugar: 500g

METHOD
Add the water and cardamom to
a saucepan over a medium heat & bring
to a boil. Stir in the sugar until fully
dissolved. Reduce the heat, cover with
a lid & simmer for about 15 minutes.
Remove from the heat and allow to cool.
Leave to infuse in the refrigerator for
3 days, then strain & bottle.
Keeps refrigerated for 3 weeks

PINE-SMOKED BLOOD ORANGE JUICE

MAKES APPROX. 200ML

—

INGREDIENTS
Blood Oranges: 6
Pine Branches: 3

METHOD
Cut the oranges in half & place in a smoker with the pine branches. Smoke for at least 30 minutes. (If you don't have a smoker, a smoking gun can be used to bubble smoke through the juice of the oranges – use pine needles in the smoking gun). Juice the orange halves & bottle.
Keeps refrigerated for 1 week

PINE CORDIAL

MAKES 200ML

—

INGREDIENTS
Pine: 5 finger-sized sprigs
Water: 200ml
Caster Sugar: about 100g
Citric Acid: Pinch

METHOD
Add the pine & water to a saucepan & heat until almost boiling. Reduce the heat & simmer for 10–15 minutes. Remove from the heat & strain; add the equivalent weight in sugar to the remaining water & stir to dissolve. Stir in the citric acid & leave to cool. Bottle.
Keeps for 1 month

SPICED GRILLED PLUM PURÉE

MAKES APPROX. 200ML

—

INGREDIENTS
Plums: 6
Cloves: 6
Ground Ginger: 1 tsp
Ground Star Anise: ½ tsp
Water: 100ml
Molasses Sugar: 75–100g (depending on the sharpness of the plums)

METHOD
Halve & de-stone the plums. Put a griddle pan over a high heat &, once hot, add the plums, flesh side down. Add the cloves, ginger & star anise. When the plums start to blacken, cover the pan with foil & turn off the heat. Leave to smoke & steam for a few minutes. Remove from the heat & put the plums & spices in a blender. Add the water & molasses sugar & blend until puréed. Pass through a fine sieve. Leave to cool, then store in a Mason jar.
Keeps refrigerated for 2 weeks

SHRUBS & SYRUPS

With a little bit of preparation & planning you can make some wonderful long & refreshing Seedlip Sodas. It's a great way to experiment, use up leftovers & make the most of the ingredients lurking in your kitchen cabinet. The basic recipe is:

SEEDLIP

+

SHRUB OR SYRUP

+

SODA

The following pages are recipes from various members of the Seedlip Team using shrubs & syrups to make tasty Seedlip Sodas.

SHRUBS

Shrubs have their origins in 17th-century England, when vinegar was used as an alternative to citrus to preserve the glut of fruits & vegetables for the off-season. Vinegar's acidic preserving properties are perfect for storing a shrub for a month in the fridge & the options are truly endless. Our shrubs are made based on this simple formula:

PLANT + VINEGAR + SUGAR + TIME = SHRUB

SYRUPS

Syrups use sugar to carry flavour. More concentrated than a cordial, a little syrup can go a very long way. Syrups when made well, keep well. Stored in the fridge, a syrup made with 1 part sugar to 1 part water should last 1 month, while a syrup made with 2 parts sugar to 1 part water should last 6 months because it's more concentrated.

PLANT + SUGAR + WATER + HEAT = SYRUP

SPICE 94
SHRUBS

SPICED BEETROOT SHRUB

KAITLIN WILKES – LONDON
MAKES 350ML

—

INGREDIENTS

Cooked Beetroot: 4
Caster Sugar: 250g
Cinnamon Sticks: 2
Cardamom Pods: 6
Black Peppercorns: 1 tsp
Cloves: 6
Apple Cider Vinegar: 100ml

METHOD

Chop the beetroot into small pieces
& place in a bowl with the sugar.
Fry the spices in a dry pan over
a medium heat until lightly toasted
& releasing an aroma. Add the toasted
spices to the beetroot & sugar & leave
to sit overnight (for a minimum of
12 hours – the longer, the better!).
Stir the sugar, beetroot & spices together
& leave for another 3–5 hours.
Pass through a sieve to remove the
spices & beetroot (but keep the beetroot
aside for garnish). Add the vinegar
to the sugar & stir, then bottle.
Keeps refrigerated for 2 months

SPICED BEETROOT COCKTAIL

—

INGREDIENTS

Spice 94: 60ml
Spiced Beetroot Shrub: 40ml
Soda: Top
Ice: Cubed
Garnish: Leftover Beetroot
Glass: Tall

METHOD

Add the Spice 94 & Spiced Beetroot
Shrub to a tall glass. Add ice & stir
quickly. Top with soda.
Garnish with beetroot.

GOLDEN HOUR SHRUB

SARAH PARNIAK – TORONTO
MAKES 450ML

—

INGREDIENTS

Anjou Pear (*see page 184*): 500g
Minced Jamaican Ginger
(*see page 185*): 1 tsp
Apple Cider Vinegar: 250ml
Sugar Syrup (*see page 186*): 250ml
Saffron Threads: 8

METHOD

Dice the pear & add to a Mason jar with
the ginger, vinegar, sugar syrup
& saffron & muddle. Leave for 36 hours.
Strain through muslin into another jar.
Keeps refrigerated for 1 month

GOLDEN HOUR COCKTAIL

—

INGREDIENTS

Spice 94: 50ml
Golden Hour Shrub: 2 tbsp
Soda: 75ml
Ice: Cubed
Garnish: Sage Leaf
Glass: Tall

METHOD

Add the Spice 94 & Golden Hour Shrub
to a tall glass over ice. Top with soda.
Garnish with a sage leaf.

K-TOWN SHRUB

AARON POLSKY – LA
MAKES APPROX. 1 LITRE

—

INGREDIENTS

Water: 425ml
Caster Sugar: 450g
Asian Pear: 100g
Fresh Root Ginger: 120g
Persimmon Vinegar: 100g
Gochugaru Chilli Flakes
(*see page 185*): 10g

METHOD

Combine the water & sugar in a bowl.
Stir until dissolved. Finely slice the pear
& ginger & add to the sugar water with
the rest of the ingredients. Leave to
infuse in a refrigerator for 24 hours.
Strain & bottle.
Keeps refrigerated for 1 month

K-TOWN COCKTAIL

—

INGREDIENTS

Spice 94: 60ml
K-Town Shrub: 20ml
Fresh Lemon Juice: 20ml
Soda: Top
Ice: Cubed
Garnish: Tangerine Segment
Glass: Tall

METHOD

Add the Spice 94, K-Town Shrub &
lemon juice to a shaker & shake. Strain
into a tall glass with ice. Top with soda.
Garnish with a tangerine segment.

SPICE 94 · SHRUBS
173

GARDEN 108
SHRUBS

PERSEPHONE SHRUB
JAMES SNELGROVE – SYDNEY
MAKES APPROX. 1.2 LITRES

—

INGREDIENTS
Cassia Quills (*see page 184*): 2
Toasted Walnuts: 25g
Persimmon: 500g
Caster Sugar: 500g
Sea Salt: 2g
Apple Cider Vinegar: 200ml

METHOD
Fry the cassia & walnuts in a dry pan
over a medium heat until lightly toasted
& releasing an aroma. Slice the
persimmon into 1cm cubes. Place the
toasted cassia & walnuts into an airtight
container with the persimmon sugar
& salt. Leave at room temperature
out of direct sunlight for 3 days.
Pass through a sieve to remove the
solids. Add the vinegar & stir. Bottle.
Keeps refrigerated for 3 weeks

PERSEPHONE COCKTAIL
—

INGREDIENTS
Garden 108: 50ml
Persephone Shrub: 25ml
Ice: Cubed
Garnish: Persimmon Wheel &
Grated Toasted Walnut
Glass: Tall

METHOD
Place the Garden 108 & Persephone
Shrub in a tall glass. Top with soda.
Garnish with a persimmon wheel
& grated toasted walnut.

LAWN GAMES SHRUB

LAURA LASHLEY – LA
MAKES 750ML

—

INGREDIENTS
Blueberries: 1kg
Dried Lemon Myrtle (*see page 185*):
4 tbsp
White Wine Vinegar: 500ml
Caster Sugar: 500g

METHOD
Add the blueberries, lemon
myrtle, vinegar & sugar to a Mason
jar & muddle. Leave for 3 days.
Gently press the berries
to extract the juice.
Fine strain & bottle.
Keeps refrigerated for 1 month

LAWN GAMES COCKTAIL

—

INGREDIENTS
Garden 108: 50ml
Lawn Games Shrub: 25ml
Fresh Lemon Juice: Dash
Soda: Top
Ice: Cubed
Garnish: Lemon Wheel
Glass: Tall

METHOD
Add the Garden 108, Lawn Games
Shrub & lemon juice to a tall glass
with ice & stir. Top with soda. Garnish
with a lemon wheel.

SUMMER SOMEWHERE

JASMIN RUTTER – AUCKLAND
MAKES 500ML

—

INGREDIENTS
Pineapple Skins: 1
Hops Pellets: 4
Thyme Sprigs: 8
Apple Cider Vinegar: 200ml
Caster Sugar: 500g
Water: 100ml

METHOD
Add the skins from 1 pineapple,
& the hops, thyme, vinegar & sugar
to a Mason jar & gently shake. Leave
for 48 hours. Strain through muslin.
Add the water & bottle.
Keeps refrigerated for 2 weeks

SUMMER SOMEWHERE COCKTAIL

—

INGREDIENTS
Garden 108: 50ml
Summer Somewhere Shrub: 25ml
Soda: Top
Ice: Cubed
Garnish: Thyme
Glass: Tall

METHOD
Pour the Garden 108 & Summer
Somewhere Shrub into a tall glass
with ice. Top with soda.
Garnish with a sprig of thyme.

GROVE 42
SHRUBS

ORANGE THEORY SHRUB

NORA FURST – SAN FRANCISCO
MAKES 700ML

—

INGREDIENTS

Fuyu Persimmon (*see page 184*): 300ml
Fresh Turmeric: 75g
Fresh Root Ginger: 75g
Caster Sugar: 200g
Pear Vinegar: 200ml
Champagne Vinegar: 200ml

METHOD

Finely dice the persimmons & discard
the green parts. Finely grate the turmeric
& ginger & add to a large Mason jar with
the persimmons & cover in the sugar.
Shake to coat & leave for 2–4 hours.
Add the vinegars & shake. Store
somewhere dark & cool for 3–9 days.
Taste & shake daily. When the flavour
is to your liking, shake hard to dissolve
any rogue granules of sugar.
Fine strain into a bottle or jar.
Keeps for 1 month

ORANGE THEORY COCKTAIL

—

INGREDIENTS

Grove 42: 50ml
Orange Theory Shrub: 20ml
Fresh Lemon Juice: Dash
Chilled Soda: Top
Ice: Cubed
Garnish: Persimmon Slice
Glass: Champagne Flute

METHOD

Place the Grove 42, Orange Theory
Shrub, lemon juice & ice in a shaker &
shake. Strain into a Champagne flute
& top with chilled soda. Press a thin
persimmon slice on to the inside
of the flute to garnish.

FRUIT & NUT
SHRUB

LUKE PEARSON – BIRMINGHAM
MAKES 500ML

—

INGREDIENTS

Frozen Cranberries: 300g
Walnuts: 200g
Caster Sugar: 250g
Apple Cider Vinegar: 250g

METHOD

Add the cranberries, walnuts & sugar
to a Mason jar & muddle well.
Add the vinegar & stir to dissolve.
Leave for 48 hours. Strain out the solids,
then fine strain into a bottle.
Keeps refrigerated for 1 month

FRUIT & NUT
COCKTAIL

—

INGREDIENTS

Grove 42: 50ml
Fruit & Nut Shrub: 25ml
Soda: Top
Ice: Cubed
Garnish: Burnt Douglas Fir
Glass: Tall

METHOD

Add the Grove 42 & Fruit & Nut Shrub
to a tall glass with ice & stir. Top with
soda. Garnish with a burnt sprig of
Douglas fir.

WOODLAND ROAD
SHRUB

STEWART HOWARD – LONDON
MAKES 500ML

—

INGREDIENTS

Juniper Berries: 10
Large Rhubarb: 2
Red Wine Vinegar: 125ml
Cider Vinegar: 125ml
Caster Sugar: 250g
Salt: Pinch

METHOD

Crush the juniper berries & add to a
Mason jar with the rhubarb, vinegars,
sugar & salt. Muddle, then leave at
room temperature for 36 hours.
Strain & bottle.
Keeps refrigerated for 1 month

WOODLAND ROAD
COCKTAIL

—

INGREDIENTS

Grove 42: 50ml
Woodland Road Shrub: 25ml
Soda: Top
Ice: Cubed
Garnish: Rhubarb Ribbon
Glass: Tall

METHOD

Add the Grove 42 & Woodland
Road Shrub to a tall glass with
ice & stir. Top with soda.
Garnish with a rhubarb ribbon.

SPICE 94
SYRUPS

TEA IN THE AFTERNOON SYRUP

LAURA LASHLEY – LA
MAKES 1 LITRE

—

INGREDIENTS

Caster Sugar: 500g
Water: 500ml
Orange Peel: 1
Lemon Peel: 1
Earl Grey Tea: 30g
Lavender Flowers: 2 tbsp

METHOD

Add the sugar, water & peels of
the orange & lemon to a saucepan
& bring to a boil. Reduce the heat
& simmer for 10–15 minutes.
Add the tea & lavender flowers
& simmer for a further 3–5 minutes.
Fine strain & leave to cool.
Keeps refrigerated for 1 month

TEA IN THE AFTERNOON COCKTAIL

—

INGREDIENTS

Spice 94: 50ml
Tea in the Afternoon Syrup: 20ml
Fresh Lemon Juice: 2 tsp
Soda: Top
Garnish: Orange Twist
Glass: Tall

METHOD

Add the Spice 94, Tea in the
Afternoon Syrup & lemon juice to
a tall glass with ice. Top with soda.
Garnish with an orange twist.

TEA & TOAST SYRUP – BREAKFAST COLLINS

CLAIRE WARNER – LONDON

MAKES APPROX. 500ML

—

INGREDIENTS

Lightly Burnt Sourdough: 100g
Muscovado Sugar: 80g
Sea Salt: Pinch
Hot Strong Black Tea: 500ml

METHOD

Place the sourdough, sugar & salt in
a food processor & blend to breadcrumbs.
Add the hot black tea & stir. Leave to
infuse for 10 minutes. Fine strain & chill.
Keeps refrigerated for 3 weeks

BREAKFAST COLLINS COCKTAIL

—

INGREDIENTS

Spice 94: 50ml
Tea & Toast Syrup: 25ml
Fresh Lemon Juice: Dash
Soda: Top
Ice: Cubed
Garnish: Lemon Wheel
Glass: Tumbler

METHOD

Add the Spice 94, Tea & Toast
Syrup & lemon juice to a tumbler
over ice. Top with soda.
Garnish with a lemon wheel.

SAGE AGAINST THE MACHINE

SEBASTIAN ROBINSON – HONG KONG

MAKES APPROX. 450ML

—

INGREDIENTS

Sage Leaves: 25g
Blueberries: 130g
Caster Sugar: 230g
Water: 230ml
Star Anise: 4

METHOD

Add the sage, blueberries, sugar &
water to a saucepan & bring to a boil.
Reduce the heat & simmer gently until
the sugar has dissolved. Muddle the
blueberries to release the juice. Add the
star anise, remove from the heat & leave
to cool. Fine strain into a glass bottle.
Keeps refrigerated for 1 month

SAGE AGAINST THE MACHINE COCKTAIL

—

INGREDIENTS

Spice 94: 50ml
Sage Against the Machine Syrup:
20ml
Soda: Top
Ice: Cubed
Garnish: Candied Sage leaf
Glass: Tall

METHOD

Add the Spice 94 & Sage Against
the Machine Syrup to a tall glass
with ice. Top with soda.
Garnish with a candied sage leaf.

GARDEN 108
SYRUPS

PROUD MARY SYRUP

NORA FURST – SAN FRANCISCO

MAKES 400ML

—

INGREDIENTS

Tomato Scraps: 100g
Beetroot Scraps: 100g
Lemon Skins: 3 (from 1 ½ lemons)
Dill: 45g
Water: 500ml
Caster Sugar: 100g
Kosher Salt: 1 tsp
Citric Acid: ¼ tsp

METHOD

Rinse & thoroughly scrub all scraps & skins. Add the dill, tomatoes & beets to a saucepan over a medium heat, cover with the water & bring to a boil. Boil for 10 minutes, or until the tomatoes begin to break down. Add the lemon skins & boil for another 3–4 minutes. Remove the lemon skins with tongs & fine strain. Press the veg with the back of a wooden spoon to squeeze out all liquid. Pass the liquid through a fine strainer to clarify. Whisk in the sugar, salt & citric acid until they dissolve. Leave to cool & bottle.
Keeps for 1 month

PROUD MARY COCKTAIL

—

INGREDIENTS

Garden 108: 50ml
Proud Mary Syrup: 2 tbsp
Soda: Top
Ice: Cubed
Garnish: Dill
Glass: Tall

METHOD

Add the Garden 108 & Proud Mary Syrup to a tall glass with ice. Top with soda. Garnish with a sprig of dill.

DOWN THE GARDEN PATH SYRUP

SARAH PARNIAK

MAKES 500ML

—

INGREDIENTS
Rhubarb: 500g
Tarragon Sprig: 1
Water: 250ml
Caster Sugar: 250g
Sea Salt: Pinch

METHOD
Dice the rhubarb & add to a saucepan
over a medium heat with the tarragon &
water & bring to a boil. Reduce the heat
& simmer gently for 10 minutes.
Add the sugar & salt & stir to dissolve.
Strain into a bottle & leave to cool.
Keeps refrigerated for 1 month

DOWN THE GARDEN PATH COCKTAIL

—

INGREDIENTS
Garden 108: 50ml
Down the Garden Path Syrup: 2 tbsp
Soda: Top
Ice: Cubed
Garnish: Tarragon
Glass: Chilled Tall

METHOD
Add the Garden 108 & Down
the Garden Path Syrup to a shaker
with ice & shake. Strain into a
chilled tall glass. Top with soda.
Garnish with a sprig of tarragon.

MELLOW YELLOW SYRUP

KAITLIN WILKES – LONDON

MAKES 400ML

—

INGREDIENTS
Bramley Apples: 4
Caster Sugar: 250g
Rosemary Sprigs: 3

METHOD
Peel 2 large Bramley apples & cut the
flesh into small 1cm cubes. Tip into a
bowl & cover with the sugar & rosemary.
Leave overnight. Juice the remaining 2
Bramley apples & add it to the bowl.
Leave to rest at room temperature for a
further night. On the third day, make
sure most of the sugar has dissolved,
then strain into a bottle.
Keeps for 1 month

MELLOW YELLOW COCKTAIL

—

INGREDIENTS
Garden 108: 50ml
Mellow Yellow Syrup: 25ml
Soda: Top
Ice: Cubed
Garnish: Rosemary
Glass: Tall

METHOD
Add the Garden 108 & Mellow
Yellow Syrup to a tall glass with ice.
Top with soda.
Garnish with a sprig of rosemary.

GARDEN 108 · SYRUPS
181

GROVE 42
SYRUPS

A LONG HARVEST SYRUP
STEWART HOWARD – LONDON
MAKES 600ML

—

INGREDIENTS
Barley: 125g
Large Figs: 4
Caster Sugar: 400g
Boiling Water: 200ml

METHOD
Dry fry the barley in a pan over a
medium heat until toasted & lightly
brown. Mash the figs & add them to the
barley. Add the sugar to the boiling water
in a saucepan & stir to dissolve. Combine
all the ingredients together & vacuum
pack (*see page 187*) for 24 hours.
Double strain & bottle.
Keeps refrigerated for 3 months

A LONG HARVEST
COCKTAIL

—

INGREDIENTS
Grove 42: 50ml
A Long Harvest Syrup: 1 tbsp
Soda: Top
Ice: Cubed
Garnish: Barley
Glass: Tumbler

METHOD
Add the Grove 42 & A Long
Harvest Syrup to a tumbler over ice.
Top with soda.
Garnish with a sprig of barley.

VENETIAN LEAF SYRUP

LUKE PEARSON – BIRMINGHAM
MAKES 1 LITRE

—

INGREDIENTS

Hot Water: 500ml
Olive Leaf Tea: 10g
Jasmine Sencha (*see page 185*): 1 tbsp
Caster Sugar: 500g

METHOD

Place the water in a saucepan and
heat to 80°C. Add the olive leaf tea
& jasmine sencha & infuse for
15 minutes. Strain into another
pan & add the sugar.
Stir to dissolve, then bottle.
Keeps refrigerated for 2 weeks

VENETIAN LEAF COCKTAIL

—

INGREDIENTS

Grove 42: 50ml
Venetian Leaf Syrup: 1 tbsp
Soda: Top
Ice: Cubed
Garnish: Orange Wedge & Olive
Glass: Wine

METHOD

Add the Grove 42 & Venetian
Leaf Syrup to a wine glass over ice.
Top with soda. Garnish with an
orange wedge & an olive.

BEACH SYRUP

BEN BRANSON – OLD AMERSHAM
MAKES ENOUGH FOR 4 LOLLIES

—

INGREDIENTS

Sea Salt: 2 pinches
Waffle Cones: 3
Vanilla Syrup: 2 tsp
Caster Sugar: 250g
Water: 250ml
Orange Natural Food Colouring:
3 drops
Fresh Orange Juice: 2 tsp

METHOD

Add all the ingredients to a saucepan
over a medium heat. Stir to dissolve.
Strain, leave to cool & bottle.
Keeps for 1 month

BEACH LOLLY

—

INGREDIENTS

Grove 42: 25ml
Beach Syrup: 1 tbsp
Soda: 25ml
Garnish: Sunshine
Glass: Lolly Mould

METHOD

Mix the Grove 42, Beach Syrup
& soda in a glass & stir. Pour
into 4 lolly moulds & freeze.
Keeps frozen for 3 months

GLOSSARY
OF INGREDIENTS & TECHNIQUES

Anjou Pear: A squat, egg-shaped pear that is particularly sweet & juicy.

Aquafaba: The viscous liquid in which legume seeds have been cooked, such as chickpeas. Due to having similar functional properties to egg whites, aquafaba can be used as an egg white replacement in some cases – a dairy-free option for sours.

Bitter Syrup: Fabri Bitter Syrup is a rich red, bitter syrup that's not the easiest to find but worth the search online. Monin Bitter Syrup is a rich red, bitter-sweet syrup.

Cascara: Meaning 'husk' or 'peel', cascara is the outer skin & pulp of a coffee cherry. It has a subtle sweetness & can be used to make sodas & syrups.

Cassia: Sometimes referred to as 'Chinese cinnamon', cassia is the aromatic bark of an East Asian tree, similar in taste to cinnamon.

Celery Seed Salt Solution: Add 50g celery salt (equal parts celery seed & sea salt) to 200ml boiling water, stir & cool.

Centrifuge: A machine with a compartment that rotates at speed, using centrifugal force to separate liquids of different densities.

Champagne Vinegar: Made from the same grapes as Champagne, this is a mild-tasting, dry white wine vinegar. Although not directly made from Champagne itself, it has to come from the Champagne region in France.

Chinois: A cone-shaped sieve with very fine mesh. Used for straining liquids or dusting fine-powdered ingredients.

Chitosan: A natural fibre product, derived from chitin, which is a substance found in the exoskeleton of shellfish, such as lobster.

Circulator/Immersion Circulator: An electrical device that heats & circulates warm fluids & maintains a selected temperature, using the sous vide (*see page 186*) method.

D'Anjou Pear Vinegar: From the D'Anjou pear, this vinegar is light in colour & has an aromatic pear flavour.

Double Strain: Use a cocktail strainer & fine tea strainer.

Droplets: We recommend Javier de las Muelas' range of non-alcoholic flavours: shop. javierdelasmuelas.com/ thedryshop/en/

Erdinger Non-alcoholic Beer: There are quite a few non-alcoholic beers available now – Erdinger's has had some great reviews.

Fee Bros Non-alcoholic Aromatic Bitters: You can buy these online & they are great additions to cocktails. They are vegetable-glycerin-based extracts that are highly concentrated & come in a range of flavours.

Fine Strain: Use a fine gauze to sift out unwanted material. Available from all good homeware stores.

Fuyu Persimmon: Native to Asia, this fruit can be eaten raw, dried or cooked & has a rich sweetness. The fruit looks similar to an orange tomato, although it is categorised as a berry.

Gochugaru Chilli Flakes:
These chilli flakes have smoky, fruity & sweet notes & originate from Korea. The flakes are an essential ingredient in kimchi & are used to give it a hot kick.

Heavy-steeped Tea: A good hour of steeping will give you a rich tea.

Honey Syrup: Made from equal quantities of honey & water – the honey is added to hot water & dissolved.

Ice: There are 3 basic kinds – cubed (regular cubed ice); block ice (a large block of ice cut to bigger cubes or columns); & crushed/pebble ice (small crushed ice).

Jamaican Ginger: Regarded as a premium variety of ginger, it is characterised by a pale-yellow inside & off-white skin. It is more aromatic than other varieties of ginger.

Jasmine Sencha: A medium-bodied tea, jasmine adds floral notes to the grassy, traditional Japanese sencha tea.

Kieselsol: A fining agent made from silicon dioxide

& used for clarifying liquids. Other fining agents are gelatin, pectinase & activated charcoal.

Lemon & Ginger Juice:
Either buy lemon juice & ginger juice & combine, or juice a lemon & fresh root ginger & combine.

Lemon Myrtle: A shrub native to the rainforests of Australia. Its leaves, when dried & crushed, add an intense lemon flavour to dishes.

Lemongrass Kombucha:
A tart & refreshing sparkling drink made from fermented tea. We recommend the one from our friends at LA Brewery.

Lemon Pelargonium Leaves: Lemon pelargonium is a herb with felt-like leaves that hold a lemon flavour & can be infused into drinks to inject citrus notes.

Malic Acid: One of the main fruit acids. Naturally occurring in apples & berries, malic acid has a tart flavour & can be found in most health food shops in powdered form.

Manuka Bark: From the manuka tree, native to New Zealand. The bark is stringy & peels in long flakes. Often used in teas & for medicinal purposes, it was made famous by the honey of the same name.

Matcha Powder: A high-quality, powdered green tea from Japan. It is finely powdered & consists of only the nutrient-rich young leaves picked from the tips of *Camellia sinensis* plants.

Microplane: A fine grater, used for zesting citrus fruits & grating nutmeg.

Mixing Glass: A piece of cocktail-making equipment used to stir & chill drinks before they are strained into the glass.

Oak Smoke Droplets:
These droplets are used to add a wood-smoked, resin flavour to food & beverages. We recommend Javier de las Muelas' Droplets.

Orange Blossom Water:
A flavouring distilled from blossoms of the orange tree. It has a soapy aroma & taste

& is excellent in food & drink in small quantities.

Pectinex Ultra SP-L: An enzyme that breaks down pectin structure. It is also an aid when clarifying juices.

Pink Peppercorn Gum Syrup: Add equal weights of pink peppercorns & sugar & water to a saucepan. Heat gently, stirring until the sugar has dissolved, then steep for 1 hour. Strain & store. Keeps for 3 months.

Powdered Kola Nut: This bitter-tasting powder is made from the nuts of the kola tree (native to Africa). It has been used as a flavouring agent in soda drinks for many years. It is the origin of the term 'cola'.

PS Lemon Myrtle Soda: Our friends at PS40 Bar in Sydney make this delicious 'Bush Tonic' with Peruvian cinchona bark, lemon & lime zest, lemongrass & lemon myrtle.

Pu'erh Tea: A variety of fermented tea produced in Yannun, China. The more aged the tea, the more earthy the aroma.

Rhubarb Soda: An intense, earthy drink. We recommend Square Root Soda, or juicing rhubarb & adding soda to make your own.

Rich Sugar Syrup: Similar to a sugar syrup, but with 2 parts sugar to 1 part water.

Royal Flush Real Kombucha: Kombucha is fermented tea & our friends at Real make a delicious Darjeeling-based 'booch'.

Sandows Cold Brew Concentrate: Coffee beans steeped cold & filtered. Friends of ours at Sandows make the best cold-brew coffee.

Shiso Leaf: Belonging to the mint family, this herb has a unique herbaceous & citrusy taste. There are green- & purple-leaved varieties, with a jagged shape & slightly prickly texture.

Sorrel Juice: Made from the petals of the sorrel plant, this juice is dark in colour & has a sour raspberry-like flavour.

Sugar Syrup: This is the simplest of sugar syrups, made with equal weights of sugar & water.

Smoker: An appliance used to infuse food or drink with smoky flavours without using heat.

Sous Vide: A heating method in which food is placed in a plastic pouch & immersed in water with a regulated temperature over a long period of time. This allows the food to cook evenly throughout while maintaining moisture.

Spindle Mix: An appliance used to speed up cocktail making. It can be used to pulse or flash-mix cocktails.

Super Bag: A very fine filter in the form of a flexible sieve. Used to strain sediment out of liquids, it can withstand high temperatures & is reusable.

Sweet & Dandy: The name of a brand of mauby syrup, which is a Caribbean drink made from mauby bark. It adds a sweet ice cream flavour to drinks & has a clove aftertaste.

Tartaric Acid: An organic substance occurring naturally in many plants & fruits, most notably in grapes, it is sour in flavour & is used as an additive to inject a sharp, tart flavour to food or drinks.

Timut Pepper: Originating from Nepal, this is a rare peppercorn with a vibrant aroma of passion fruit & grapefruit. If eaten it leaves a tingling sensation in your mouth for a few minutes.

Tincture: Alcohol extracts from herbs & plants in a solution, often used for medicinal purposes.

Tonka Bean Droplets: The tonka bean is the flat, dark, wrinkled seed from giant cumaru trees in South America. These fragrant droplets inject a complex sour cherry, clove and cinnamon taste to cocktails. We recommend Javier de las Muelas' Droplets, which are glycerine-based, non-alcoholic flavours.

Top: A quantity of carbonated liquid, roughly equivalent to 50–100ml, used in cocktail making to finish the drink.

Twist & Sparkle Bottle: Used to carbonate alcoholic & non-alcoholic drinks using a plastic operating element fuelled by a carbon dioxide charger, it adds carbonation directly into the drink.

Vacuum Pack: A method of packaging that removes air from inside the package before sealing, thus removing oxygen & extending shelf life.

Vanilla Peanut Milk: Add 250g unsalted, roasted peanuts to 500ml water & soak for 6 hours. Place the peanuts, 750ml water, 2 dates & ½ tsp vanilla extract into a blender & blend for 1 minute. Strain using muslin cloth.

Vegetable Glycerine: A clear liquid produced from plant oils. Often used as a replacement for alcohol in herbal & botanical tinctures, it adds sweetness to drinks.

Wattleseed: A nutritious, roasted seed from the acacia shrub, originating in Australia. The distinctive coffee, chocolate & hazelnut flavour means wattleseed can be used in both savoury & sweet dishes.

Yuzu: A citrus fruit from Japan with a distinct sourness & taste similar to grapefruit & lime mixed together. The yuzu is the size of a tangerine & is used for its juice & aromatic rind.

INDEX

A

All the Spice 18
almond milk: Milk Punch 150
apple juice: Garden Collins
 102
 Garden Sour 88
apples: Mellow Yellow Syrup
 181
apricots *see* Spiced Apricot
 Ceylon Shrub
Avocado Pit Honey 122
 Goin' Bush 116

B

Barbarelless 114
barley: A Long Harvest Syrup
 182
 Malt Syrup 166
Beach Syrup 183
 Beach Lolly 183
beetroot: Proud Mary Syrup
 180
 Spiced Beetroot Shrub 172
bergamot purée: Tealip 100
Bitter Aperitif, Non-alcoholic
 64
 Nogroni® 40
Blossom 148
blueberries: Sage Against the
 Machine 179
Blueberry Shrub 120
Bonfire Glyncture 166
 Malt 134
Breakfast Collins Cocktail 179
Breeze Field 54
Buttermilk Vinaigrette 123
 Snap! 112

C

The Cabin in the Grove 162
Cardamom Syrup 169
Carrot Cordial 166
 Peel 132
Cascara Syrup 167
 Cascara 142
Cashew Punch 154
Celeriac Root Tincture 66
 Root Cellar 58
Celeriac Syrup 66
 Root Cellar 58
Celery Root & Cinnamon
 Cordial 65
 Pais de la Canela 52
chamomile tea: Spice &
 Everything Nice 50
Champagne vinegar: Orange
 Theory Shrub 176
Cider Spice Noir Tea:
 Pais de la Canela 52
Citrus 144
Clements 140
Cloudberry Cordial:
 Tallstrunt 60
Cocanela 46
coconut milk: Cocanela 46
cordials: Carrot Cordial 166
 Celery Root & Cinnamon
 Cordial 65
 G&Tea Cordial 120
 Orchard Cordial 118
 Pine Cordial 169
 Rooibos & Turmeric
 Cordial 167
 Spiced Peach Cordial 67
cranberries: Fruit & Nut
 Shrub 177

Cucumber & Lemon Shrub 119
 Cucumber 94
Cut Grass Glyncture 118

D

Down the Garden Path Syrup
 181
 Down the Garden Path
 Cocktail 181
Dragon Fruit Syrup 123
 Tuffnut's Tonic 110
Droplets 184

E

Earl Grey Tea: Tea in the
 Afternoon Syrup 178
Elderflower Lemon Sherbet
 120
 Garden Collins 102
Eliza 22
Endothermic Verjus 119
 Sage 92
Erdinger Non-alcoholic Beer:
 Winter Shandy 56
Espresso Martino® 34

F

Fabri Bitter Syrup: Non-
 alcoholic Bitter Aperitif 64
Fruit & Nut Shrub 177
 Fruit & Nut Cocktail 177

G
G&Tea Cordial 120
  Tealip 100
Garden 108 10
  cocktails 68–123
  shrub sodas & syrups
    174–5, 180–1
Garden Booch 80
Garden Collins 102
Garden Sour 88
Garden Spritz 86
Ginger 20
ginger: K-Town Shrub 173
ginger ale/beer: Ginger 20
  Thoroughbred 136
  Wood 138
Ginger & Pumpkin Shrub 64
  Pumpkin 28
ginger cordial: Cashew Punch
  154
glynctures: Bonfire Glyncture
  166
  Cut Grass Glyncture 118
  Sage Glyncture 119
Goin' Bush 116
Golden Hour Shrub 173
  Golden House Cocktail 173
Gorse & Beeswax Shrub 168
  Honey 152
grapefruit: Maple Faux
  Vermouth 65
Grapefruit & Chilli Syrup 123
  Barbarelless 114
grapefruit juice: Clarified
  Pink Grapefruit Juice 121
  Islands in the Stream #1970
    104
  Mr Howard 38
grapes: Ompressed White
  Grapes 122–3
grass: Cut Grass Glyncture
  118

Grass is Greener 82
Green Yard 164
Grove 42 10
  cocktails 124–69
  shrub sodas & syrups 176–7,
    182–3

H
Honey 152
honey: Gorse & Beeswax
  Shrub 168
  Noddy 32
honey syrup: Cocanela 46
  Peas & Flowers 106
  Squirrel Nut Fizz 158

I
In-a-Gadda-da-Vida 108
Islands in the Stream #1970 104

K
K-Town Shrub 173
  K-Town Cocktail 173
Kola Nut Tea 64
  Melondramatic 44
kombucha: Garden Booch 80
  Spice Booch 24

L
Lapsang Souchong tea:
  Bonfire Glyncture 166
Lawn Games Cocktail 175
Lawn Games Shrub 175
lemon & lime soda: Citrus 144
Lemon Balm Vinegar 121
  Peas & Flowers 106
lemon juice: Garden Collins
  102

Green Yard 164
Milk Punch 150
Mr Howard 38
Noddy 32
Winter Shandy 56
see also Cucumber & Lemon
  Shrub; Elderflower Lemon
  Sherbet; Maple Faux
  Vermouth
lemon myrtle soda:
  Melondramatic 44
Lime 90
lime juice: Barbarelless 114
lollies: Beach Lolly 183
A Long Harvest Syrup 182
  A Long Harvest Cocktail 182

M
Malt Syrup 166
  Malt 134
mandarin juice: Honey 152
Mango 146
Mango Drops 167
Mangosteen Juice 121
  Islands in the Stream #1970
    104
Maple Faux Vermouth 65
  Something in the Way 48
marmalade: Eliza 22
Meadow Syrup 118
  Grass is Greener 82
Mellow Yellow Syrup 181
  Mellow Yellow Cocktail 181
Melondramatic 44
milk: Cashew Punch 154
  Milk Punch 150
Mr Howard 38
Mr McGregor 84
Monin Bitter Syrup:
  Non-alcoholic Bitter
    Aperitif 64

N

Nettle & Pear Shrub 119
Sage 92
Noddy 32
Nogroni® 40
Nothing Rhymes with
Orange 130

O

Ompressed White Grapes
122–3
orange juice: Blossom 148
see also Pine-smoked Blood
Orange Juice; Rectified
Orange Juice
Orange Theory Shrub 176
Orange Theory Cocktail 176
Orchard Cordial 118
Orchard Spritz 78

P

Pais de la Canela 52
Pea & Eucalyptus Soda 122
Goin' Bush 116
Spiced Peach Cordial 67
peanuts: Vanilla Peanut Milk
168
Pear & Kaffir Lime Syrup 121
In-a-Gadda-da-Vida 108
Pear Vinegar: Orange Theory
Shrub 176
pears: Golden Hour Shrub 173
K-Town Shrub 173
Nettle & Pear Shrub 119
Peas & Flowers 106
Peas & Love 74
Peel 132
Persephone Shrub 174
Persephone Shrub Cocktail
174

persimmons: Orange Theory
Shrub 176
Persephone Shrub 174
Pine Cordial 169
The Cabin in the Grove 162
Pine-Smoked Blood Orange
Juice 168
The Cabin in the Grove 162
Pine Tree Syrup 67
Tallstrunt 60
pineapple skins: Summer
Somewhere 175
Pineapple Tepache 67
Pineapple 30
plums: Spiced Grilled Plum
Purée 169
Proud Mary Syrup 180
Proud Mary Cocktail 180
PS Lemon Myrtle Soda:
Melondramatic 44
Puff Pastry Cream 122
In-a-Gadda-da-Vida 108
Pumpkin 28
Ginger & Pumpkin Shrub
64

R

Rectified Orange Juice 66
Breeze Field 54
Rectified Watermelon Juice
65
Melondramatic 44
rhubarb: Down the Garden
Path Syrup 181
Woodland Road Shrub 177
rhubarb soda: Barbarelless 114
Rooibos & Turmeric Cordial
167
Milk Punch 150
Root Cellar 58
Rosemary Dust 168

S

Sage 92
Sage Against the Machine 179
Sage Against the Machine
Cocktail 179
Sage Glyncture 119
Sandows Cold Brew
Concentrate: Espresso
Martino® 34
sherbet: Elderflower Lemon
Sherbet 120
shrubs 11, 170–9
Cucumber & Lemon Shrub
119
Fruit & Nut Shrub 177
Ginger & Pumpkin Shrub
64
Golden Hour Shrub 173
Gorse & Beeswax Shrub 168
K-Town Shrub 173
Nettle & Pear Shrub 119
Orange Theory Shrub 176
Persephone Shrub 174
Spiced Apricot Ceylon
Shrub 66
Spiced Beetroot Shrub 172
Sugar Snap Shrubmakes 118
Watermelon & Basil Shrub
120
Snap! 112
Something in the Way 48
sorrel juice: Non-alcoholic
Sweet Vermouth 64
sourdough: Tea & Toast
Syrup Breakfast Collins 179
Souverian 62
Spice 94 10, 12–67
cocktails 16, 18–41
shrub sodas & syrups 172–3,
178–9
Spice & Everything Nice 50
Spice Booch 24

Spice Martino® 36
Spiced Apricot Ceylon Shrub
66
Winter Shandy 56
Spiced Beetroot Shrub 172
Spiced Beetroot Cocktail 172
Spiced Grilled Plum Purée 169
Spiced Peach Cordial 67
Souverian 62
Sqirl 160
Squirrel Nut Fizz 158
Sugar Snap Pea Syrup 123
Sugar Snap Shrubmakes
118
Mr McGregor 84
Summer Somewhere 175
Summer Somewhere
Cocktail 175
Sunshine Syrup 166
Clements 140
Sweet Vermouth, Non-
alcoholic 64
Nogroni® 40
syrups 11, 170–1, 180–3
Beach Syrup 183
Cascara Syrup 167
Celeriac Syrup 66
Down the Garden Path
Syrup 181
Dragon Fruit Syrup 123
Grapefruit & Chilli Syrup
123
A Long Harvest Syrup 182
Malt Syrup 166
Meadow Syrup 118
Mellow Yellow Syrup 181
Pear & Kaffir Lime Syrup
121
Pine Tree Syrup 67
Proud Mary Syrup 180
Sugar Snap Pea Syrup 123
Sunshine Syrup 166

Tea & Toast Syrup Breakfast
Collins 179
Tea in the Afternoon Syrup
178

T
Tallstrunt 60
Tea & Toast Syrup Breakfast
Collins 179
Tea in the Afternoon Syrup
178
Tea in the Afternoon
Cocktail 178
Tealip 100
Thoroughbred 136
Timut Pepper: Bonfire
Glyncture 166
tincture: Celeriac Root
Tincture 66
tomato scraps: Proud Mary
Syrup 180
Tuffnut's Tonic 110

V
Vanilla 26
Vanilla Peanut Milk 168
verjus: Garden Spritz 86
Non-alcoholic Sweet
Vermouth 64
Root Cellar 58
Souverian 62
Spice Martino® 36
Yuzu Verjus 167
see also Endothermic Verjus
Venetian Leaf Cocktail 183
Venetian Leaf Syrup 183
vinaigrette: Buttermilk
Vinaigrette 123
vinegar: Lemon Balm
Vinegar 121

W
waffle cones: Beach Syrup 183
walnuts: Fruit & Nut Shrub
177
Watermelon & Basil Shrub
120
Watermelon 96
watermelon juice:
Melondramatic 44
Rectified Watermelon Juice
65
wine: Orchard Spritz 78
Winter Shandy 56
Wood 138
Woodland Road Shrub 177
Woodland Road Cocktail
177

yuzu juice: Sqirl 160
Yuzu Verjus 167
Mango 146

ACKNOWLEDGEMENTS

Thanks first must go to the Penguin Random
House team & specifically Lizzy Goudsmit. Your
belief in us & what we're doing means a lot!

To the designers at Smith & Gilmour:
thank you for laying this out so beautifully.

To Jo Roberts-Miller: thank you for such
a meticulous copy-edit.

To Rob Lawson, whose exquisite photography
adorns these pages & who has been with me since
day one: Rob, this is as much your book as it is ours.

To the guys at Pearlfisher for your stunning
illustration work & continued expertise in bringing
Seedlip to life: thank you.

To my team: thank you for your hard work, drive
& determination. I couldn't do this without you.

Stewart, Kait, Luke, Lucinda & Ben:
we smashed the shoots, you're legends!

To Agung, Aidan, Alex, Anya, Chris, Dev, Devon,
Erik, Giacomo, Iain, Jack, Jim, Jimmy, Josh, Luke,
Matt, Michael, Nicholas, Ryan, Rob, Robin, Tess,
Thor, Xav: thank you so much for your support
& wonderful recipes, guys. I think it's testament to
you & hopefully to Seedlip that I was able to brief
you all at the same time, with no overlap, no
rebriefing & such diversity in your drinks.